The Same River Twice

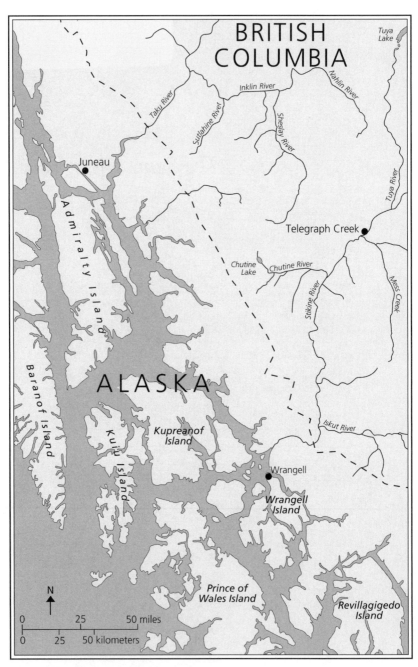

The Chutine, Stikine, and Sheslay rivers

The Same River Twice

A Boatman's Journey Home

MICHAEL D. BURKE

The University of Arizona Press

Tucson

The University of Arizona Press
© 2006 Michael D. Burke

♾ This book is printed on acid-free, archival-quality paper.
Manufactured in the United States of America

11   10   09   08   07   06   6   5   4   3   2   1

Library of Congress Cataloging-in-Publication Data

Burke, Michael D., 1953–
    The same river twice : a boatman's journey home /
Michael D. Burke.
       p. cm.
    Includes bibliographical references.
    ISBN-13: 978-0-8165-2531-7 (pbk. : alk. paper)
    ISBN-10: 0-8165-2531-5 (pbk. : alk. paper)
    1. Alaska—Description and travel. 2. British Columbia
—Description and travel. 3. Rivers–Alaska. 4. Rivers—
British Columbia. 5. Burke, Michael D., 1953—Travel—
Alaska. 6. Burke, Michael D., 1953—Travel—British
Columbia. 7. Barrington, Sid, d. 1963—Travel. 8. Boats
and boating—Alaska. 9. Boats and boating—British
Columbia. I. Title.
    F910.5.B87   2006
    917.9804'5—dc22
2006006340

Publication of this book is made possible in part by the proceeds of a permanent endowment created with the assistance of a Challenge Grant from
the National Endowment for the Humanities, a federal agency.

For Pat, who let me go, then let me come back.

And for all the guides who ever were.

Do I contradict myself?

Very well, then, I contradict myself

—Walt Whitman, "Song of Myself"

Contents

Acknowledgments

I want to thank my wife, Patricia O'Donnell, for her unfailing support and assistance with this book. She walked the difficult tightrope between enthusiasm and correction, always honest in each. I also must thank Bob Kimber, who read a "final" draft of this—which turned out to be an early draft—and who provided suggestions and enough encouragement to keep going. And Adam Tanous, who understood what I was after and saw flaws that I hadn't been able to bring myself to recognize as flaws: not bad editing for a river guide. All infelicities and flaws are my creation; any virtues the book has wouldn't be as numerous without the help of those three readers.

Some characters' names have been changed, including "Max." In each case, I changed the name only because I thought it unfair to name and characterize someone who didn't have a chance to object. For those whose real names appear here, I hope you're flattered by the portrait—if not, too bad.

An early version of parts of chapters 10 and 11 appeared in the December 2000 issue of *Organization and Environment*.

BOOK I *Chutine*

That wave's been standing off this jut of shore

Ever since rivers, I was going to say,

Were made in heaven.

   —Robert Frost, "West-Running Brook"

The face of the water, in time, became a wonderful book—

a book that was a dead language to an uneducated passenger,

but which told its mind to me without reserve, delivering its most

cherished secrets as clearly as if it uttered them with a voice.

   —Mark Twain, *Life on the Mississippi*

1 *Load Up*

The rivers flow not past, but through us, thrilling, tingling, vibrating every
fiber and cell of the substance of our bodies, making them glide and sing.
— John Muir, *John of the Mountains*

"Say the word, 'death.'"
"Death."
"Say the word, 'love.'"
"Love."
"Say the word, 'hate.'"
"Hate."
"Say the word, 'pain.'"
"Pain."
"Say the word, 'hope.'"

～～

The audiologist's testing room was in an old stone building in Waterloo,
Iowa: a quiet, dark, cool room in spite of the searing summer heat outside. I repeated the words as he checked the damage in my right ear, whose
drum had been ruptured, it turned out, during horseplay the day before at
a motel pool along the wasteland of Interstate 80 in Ohio.

We had arrived at the motel after a two-day drive from Maine in the
family station wagon. Among other things, the station wagon held my river
gear and a folding sea kayak. Half of the kayak rode on the roof; the other

half was inside, taking up too much space among the suitcases, two teen-agers, my pregnant wife, and me.

As I sat in the chair, headphones on my ears, this all seemed foolish, as though I were kidding: the station wagon, the motel, Interstate 80, the pool, the audiologist. I would never get to where Sid had been from here.

Inside his glass booth, the audiologist read from a list. I felt like his pris-oner, trapped in this incantatory poem, my punishment to chant this con-fession, whose theme was a mixture of universal and particular, emotions and things, fears and hopes.

"Say the word, 'boat.'"

"Boat."

"Say the word, 'pool.'"

"Pool."

"Say the word, 'fool.'"

"Fool."

"Say the word, 'shout.'"

"Shout."

The night before, when I'd been awakened by the throbbing pain in my ear, I had tried various ways to relieve it. I even lay for a time with my head hanging off the side of the bed. Later, I went into the bathroom to get some tissue, thinking that would hold the ear canal open and let the water drain.

It was about three a.m. when I tiptoed in and flipped on the light. All motel mirrors are unforgiving, but this one was unusually cruel. It showed a man who was too old for this sort of thing, nearly bald, with a graying beard and bags under his eyes; with a two-inch scar on his arm where an itchy black mole, a melanoma, had been removed nine months before; with his wife behind him in the other room, a round mound in the bed, seven months pregnant. It was not the reflection of a man who should be head-ing into wild places.

I was awake most of the night, struggling with the pain in my ear and the symbolism it held for the journey. Symbolism still unresolved, I fell asleep, and the water behind the eardrum drained out. In the morning we awoke to another sweltering day. Tired and in pain, I drove the station wagon six hundred more miles to my wife's hometown in northeastern Iowa. The first thing I did when we arrived at her parents' house was knock a mirror off their wall, shattering it into a thousand pieces. More symbolism.

Say the word, "young."
Say the word, "past."
Say the word, "regret."
Say the word, "water."
Say the word, "river."
River.

2 *Swift-Water Pilots*

*... all pilots are tireless talkers, when gathered together, and as they talk
only about the river they are always understood and always interesting.
Your true pilot cares nothing about anything on earth but the river ...*
    —Mark Twain, *Life on the Mississippi*

From Maine to Parkersburg, Iowa, in the summer of 1991 was a long step
taken in the footsteps of a man sometimes called "The Champion Swift-
Water Pilot of the North" but usually known as Sid. Sid, Sidney C. Barrington, earned the swift-water title as a riverboat captain on the Yukon River
during the Klondike Gold Rush of 1898 and, later, on the Stikine River in
British Columbia. Sid wasn't the most famous captain on the Yukon, or
the best, but he was the only one who was a distant relative of mine: his
mother and my great-great-grandmother were sisters. And we had a connection through Whidbey Island in Puget Sound, where Sid was born and
where I spent the best parts of my summers for many years.

But this alone wouldn't have gotten me on the road north, if it hadn't
been for another relationship. In 1973, ten years after Sid died and eighteen
years after his last journey down the Stikine, I dropped out of college in
Berkeley, became a whitewater river guide, and devoted the next ten years
to running rivers in the West.

It wasn't until I had been guiding for a few years that I heard about
Sid, and then I was charmed that the two of us, descendants of the same
Anglo-Irish immigrants, should be involved in the same odd profession. As

I heard more about him, I was impressed by his complete devotion to moving water, impressed that someone of his generation could have had such a passion for rivers.

My own passion began on an early morning in 1973, when I woke from a jostling nap in an old pickup truck on a rutted dirt road and looked out the window, down into the canyon of the Stanislaus River in northern California, where the river was deep green and white. "Is that it?" I asked the two other men in the truck, Brent and Tim, who, like me, were training to be guides. "There she is," replied Brent, and we pulled off the road to look. There was a distant sound rising out of the canyon, a sound that combined many: rumbling, hissing, a whoosh, a whisper almost of wind. "Cool," I said, looking down. The other two laughed. "Cold," Tim noted, for it was late March in California; snow was still packed on the tallest ridges I could see upstream, and the river would be bitter.

For eleven years I spent all of my summers—and parts of the spring and fall—guiding on rivers, from the Brooks Range of Alaska to Mexico. Then I moved on to other things: graduate school, marriage, teaching, parenting. Now, in Parkersburg, I was thirty-eight. I guided a little every year, but it was my past, not my future, even if in a weird way I still thought of myself as a guide, temporarily masquerading as professor, father, writer. When I was away from rivers I missed them, the sensations, the contact with wild places, yet each year I drifted further away from them and from guiding. I wrote essays and articles about the guiding life, a way of trying to hold onto the experience, and I had an idea that I might try a longer work some day—maybe call it "Child of Glaciers," after a phrase Sid used once in reference to the Stikine.

By 1991 Sid was drifting away, too. The people who had known him were dying, the traces of him fading. Before it was all gone, before both guiding and Sid were so far away that I could never get back to them, I wanted to make one more run. And the ideal place to go was where Sid had been. Perhaps I could understand my own affection for rivers, or I could honor his, or I could put a proper end to my guiding days if I made this pilgrimage to British Columbia and Alaska. I had many reasons for going, I told myself and anyone who asked. But I knew the trip was also an excuse to see new waters, when my opportunities for such visitations were dwindling—there were too many things that stood in the way, and the baby and the melanoma were the ultimate signs that my time on rivers had nearly passed.

—————

Summer days in Parkersburg alternate between high humidity and rain—there is always moisture in the air, sometimes suspended, sometimes falling. I sat on my in-laws' deck overlooking the town park, going for runs through the cornfields in the oppressive air, drinking beer in the late afternoon, and savoring the slow, simple nature of a visit to Parkersburg, Iowa. Then I called pilots in Alaska.

My plan for the trip was vague—I knew only that I should return to the wildest parts of the area Sid had traveled for thirty-five years in northern, interior British Columbia. Beyond that, what I would do was still unclear.

I had studied maps all winter and saw this: one of the major tributaries of the Stikine is the Chutine River, coming down from the north and west in a sinuous curve. About eight miles up the Chutine from the confluence with the Stikine, the Barrington River enters from the north, and in the elbow formed by the conjunction of the Barrington River and the Chutine is Mt. Barrington. I contacted the Canadian Ministry of Names, to be sure this was the right Barrington. It was: "Barrington River was first known as 'First North Fork of Clearwater Creek,' then as Barrington Creek; named for Captain Sidney C. Barrington and his brother, Hill, prospectors and owners of the Barrington Transportation Company of Wrangell, Alaska."

These eponymous forms were places I should get to—touching them would be talismanic, I thought. I could hire a float plane and fly into Chutine Lake, a long, thin lake filling a valley that appeared on maps to be bordered by glaciers and lofty peaks. I would then hike up Chutine Creek, which feeds the lake, and after a couple of miles leave that drainage and turn to the east, passing over a saddle that separates the drainage of the Chutine from the headwaters of the Barrington River. Then, after only another eight miles, I would reach the glacial headwaters of the Barrington and begin a float by raft there. I would travel downstream on the Barrington about twenty miles, until it curled around the eastern flank of Mt. Barrington and met Jimmie Creek, where I would stop and climb the mountain. After descending I would run the rest of the Barrington, join the Chutine, float out to the Stikine, and follow it all the way into Wrangell.

Clearly this was insane. It was the kind of plan one comes up with while sitting in one's living room in the middle of winter, a continent and half a year removed from the reality of living out the plan.

From Iowa I called a bush pilot in Wrangell and described what I needed. At first he was skeptical. But as the idea caught hold, as it always does with bush pilots, he managed to convince himself it was possible, until finally he was saying, to himself more than to me, "Yeah, you could take the door off the 207, and get rid of the copilot's seat, and tip the plane up on one wing, and just push the raft out the door. Yeah, that would work."

This sounded reasonable to me, too! We would put the raft in the front seat of the 207 next to the pilot, and he and I would fly over the tail-end of a glacier, he'd tip the plane up, and I would give my poor old raft a kick out the door and watch it bounce along the shore and hope it didn't bounce into the river and vanish. This seemed like a sober and practical idea, at least in Iowa.

I even had a second plan. Another river, the Sheslay, drains the area to the north of the Barrington River, its headwaters a glacier or two away from the headwaters of the Barrington. The Sheslay travels a complicated route: it exits east from the mountains and north, in the opposite direction from the Chutine, then meets the Hackett, where it continues roughly north, becomes the Inklin River while making a left turn to the west, merges into the Taku River, and travels west and south into Taku Arm, which enters Stephens Passage south of Juneau. I could land on Chutine Lake, hike over into the valley of the Sheslay, where we would have dropped the raft, and float out that way. This plan was as impossible as the first one, but I considered it.

One path would allow me to touch the totemic grounds and waters of the Barrington River and Mt. Barrington and to exit via the Stikine. The other would be a wilder journey, exploring new territory—few people had ever been down the Sheslay, I knew, and by going that direction I could leave my raft where Taku River became Taku Arm and switch there to a sea kayak for the sixty-mile paddle into Juneau. Going by the Sheslay there would be three different forms of travel: hiking and climbing, rafting, and sea kayaking. I liked that idea. It might be the proper response to Sid's legacy. A wilderness triathlon, as though this were a competition and I was going to score points with the ghost of Sid through this frenzy of bush activities.

I wouldn't be going by myself. Solo trips in the bush are a bad idea, and I had generated enough bad ideas by myself as it was. When I decided that the summer of 1991 was the time, I called one of my guiding friends, Dennis Eagan, in Anchorage. Denny was a sweet-natured guy, then in his early forties, who had devoted himself to the outdoors life. He had been a river guide, a ski patrolman, and a sea kayaking guide and had run wilderness trips for teenage hoodlums. Denny was married once, but even that had been sacrificed to his need for wilderness. I knew Denny would be interested.

I reached Denny and made my pitch: three weeks in wild parts of B.C. and Alaska. Denny would have been perfect, since in addition to his wilderness skills, he also has a reflective streak that would have led to some wonderfully morbid conversations about how screwed up everything is, including our lives. But Denny was going to be sea kayaking in Glacier Bay during the time I needed to go. Then, trying to be helpful, he said, "But hey, there's a guy on my couch who might be interested," and he passed the phone to a friend of his.

I described my plan to the man on the couch, Max Sodalis, and within ten minutes he was ready to go. He sounded like a good fit. He was a climber, had committed various types of adventure—including sea kayaking in the South Pacific—and he sounded bright and cheerful and enthusiastic, failings which I was willing to overlook. He had also never run whitewater.

Max was a biologist, working that summer on a project aboard a research vessel cruising Alaskan waters. Most important, he was available. I would meet him in Juneau on the early morning of July first, not knowing much about him, not even what he looked like.

Somehow I was able to justify leaving my wife, Patricia, who was more than seven months pregnant, to take care of our other two children (hers, my stepchildren, but I was the only father they'd ever known), so that I could disappear into the bush for three weeks. Even worse, she had fractured her tailbone the morning we left Maine, so she was in considerable pain, especially while sitting, which, hugely pregnant, is all she wanted to do. And she was in Parkersburg to visit her mother, who was struggling to live with chronic myelogenic leukemia.

I brazened it out, pretending there wasn't anything outrageous about such abandonment. She had said I could go, and I jumped at the permission, even though she thought the trip was a kind of "death wish." It wasn't, but my desperation, created by my sense of time slipping away, overwhelmed my conscience. I ignored my obligations, dismissed the need to come up with better reasons for leaving. I would be back promptly in three weeks, I told her, whole in body and satisfied in spirit, well before the baby was due.

Sheepishly, I left Iowa for California, where I bought supplies, shipped my raft and sea kayak off to Wrangell, and made more phone calls to Alaska. I finally reached the pilot who would fly us in, a man named Dan Baldwin. I asked him about using the 185 to fly us to a gravel bar on the headwaters of the Sheslay, if there were such a bar. Dan said he couldn't because they had only one plane now, and it was rigged as a float plane.

What happened to the other one?

"I was taking it down to Ketchikan and the engine blew up," he said.

And then? "Well, I put it down on the water and waited. Sat there for an hour and a half, and just when a boat was pulling up to give me a tow, the damn plane rolled over and sank. But I was able to step from the pontoon onto the boat without getting my toes wet."

Dan sounded like the man for my job. We agreed on some harebrained plan using a different plane, which I knew would never unfold in the way we had planned it.

I flew north to Juneau and took a taxi out to the Alaska Ferry Terminal at Auk Bay. Max was coming in on a ferry from Skagway at three in the morning, and we would reboard it for the trip down to Wrangell. Even at eleven p.m. the sky was light enough to read by, and I settled into a familiar position, the traveler's position—sprawled on your luggage—and I felt a part of old routines. Hanging out, sprawling, waiting: waiting for planes, for trains, for friends, for money, for the mood, for the sun, for night, for a ride. I was a little out of practice, after my sedentary academic life, but my butt soon adjusted to the correct posture for leaning against a river bag, as though I were a guide.

The ferry pulled in at a quarter to three. At three, cars began leaving the ferry, including the black Chevy van I had been told to watch for. With the sky beginning to lighten around Juneau, I got my first look at my companion. He had a three-days' growth of beard, thinning brown hair pulled back into a skinny ponytail, and a moustache, and he was wearing heavy denim carpenter's pants and a chamois shirt. He was about five foot nine, stocky, with glasses. Even in the middle of the night he seemed cheerful.

We had to reboard the ferry soon, so we pawed quickly through the equipment in his van. There was one sport coat hanging up—for interviews, he said—but the rest of the van was devoted to carabiners, fleece and pile garments, a mountain bike, maps. Max plucked the things he needed, including a short-barreled shotgun—a form of bear protection—and climbing helmets and ice axes.

We boarded, stored the gear, and found our berth. This was the second time I had taken an Alaskan ferry; the first time had been fourteen years before, when another river guide and I hitchhiked the seven hundred miles from Fairbanks to Skagway to catch one. We had been stuck overnight in Tok Junction on the Alaskan Highway, but we'd still made Skagway with just enough time to buy a bottle of whiskey and board with a crowd of other young people.

By five I was fast asleep, lulled by the motion of the ferry and the sound of the engines. I slept until noon. When I woke up, Max was gone, and after a shower I went in search of him, thinking it was time to get acquainted. I got a cup of coffee and took a seat near a window overlooking the Inside Passage. The vision, of mountains that go straight up from the sea, and clouds that cut them off, and the smooth water of the passage, reminded me that I wasn't in Iowa anymore.

Max found me at the window and we talked, the talk of two men getting acquainted. He was divorced, and his two sons lived with him one year and the next with their mother wherever she might be in the South. Max had gotten a Ph.D. in biology from the University of Wyoming and taught at Penn State but stepped off the academic track to be mobile. He had taken high school teaching jobs in a number of exotic locations, his priority being not the job but the location, it seemed. He had taught in the Marshall Islands, in the Aleutians, and in Montana and Wyoming. He was a true wilder-guy, the sort of fellow who has quit ordinary life to go to the wild places.

Max went to take a nap, and I spent the next two hours in the cafeteria, going over my notes for the trip, trying to decide which of the stupid plans

I had made was the least stupid. In midafternoon we docked in Wrangell. It was raining—no surprise—the clouds hanging low, almost right on top of the water.

Wrangell is on an island in a glorious setting, which one could appreciate if it weren't always masked by rain and clouds. I had been there once before, when the clouds unexpectedly parted and lifted, and the sun shone down between them like a benediction. Islands appeared in the Sound— little furred humps—as did the glaciers at the mouth of the Stikine, and more glaciers in the LeConte Glacier area, and the improbably steep mountains lining the mainland shore.

Because of the clouds, we hadn't been able to see the mouth of the Stikine as we ferried past it on our way into town. This meant we probably wouldn't fly out that day. At the ferry terminal we unloaded our mountain of gear, and I called Dan Baldwin. I was right in thinking we wouldn't fly. After I hung up I looked at our pile of equipment and plunged into despair. There was too much, and it added to the growing feeling I hadn't planned all of this very well.

I called around and got us a room, then phoned the airline to make sure the raft and kayak had arrived. They assured me it was all there, everything was fine. Max and I shoved the offensive gear pile against a wall of the ferry terminal and walked into town. We browsed, stopped for a pizza, then settled into a booth at an ice cream shop and talked. Max was a devotee of the new Men's Movement, and he liked to talk about it—a lot. I foresaw conflict, as there had been with another enthusiastic person, a guide friend from Alaska days, Bo Mandeville. Bo had been guiding for a long time, since 1970 or so, most often on the Colorado. He was an interesting, wild, slightly off-center guy, who was a legend in rafting circles for his dangerous stunts.

Once, Bo was running the Rogue River in Oregon and stopped to scout Rainey Falls. Rainey is an awful, boiling place. It is a portion of a rock intrusion that the river passes over and through; the river drops about ten feet, straight down, with the added problem of sheer rock walls on either side that force the water back on itself. The power of the water coming over the falls is tremendous, and the water is so aerated by the turbulence and recirculation that it won't hold anything up: a log going over the falls disappears immediately out of sight, then reappears forty or fifty feet downstream, where the current resurfaces. On my first two runs down the Rogue, I rode rafts over the falls but, having survived, decided life was precious and never tried it again.

While Mandeville was scouting the normal run, through a midchannel around the falls, someone's dog swam out into the river to chase a stick and couldn't return to shore before being swept over the falls. The shore was lined with guides and passengers, and they all watched, horrified, as the poor dog, realizing it wasn't going to get to shore, turned to face downstream and paddled into the foam. No doubt there were gasps and oohs and maybe a stifled shriek or two, and a collective hurrah when the dog popped up fifty feet downstream and swam to shore, where it vomited. Then it walked up to the falls, sat, and stared.

Most people would take the dog's run as a cautionary lesson. Not Mandeville. He took it as a sign of possibilities, and he managed to talk Denny Eagan into joining him on a swim. They put on two life jackets apiece, hopped into the water, and swam over the falls. According to Mandeville, the swim "wasn't bad."

Mandeville was prone to mood changes: his highs were Olympian, his lows subterranean. He was one of the first people involved with est, the egregious personal growth movement started in San Francisco. Mandeville got me to guide once on a river trip for est leaders, including Werner Erhard, the founder of est. At times Mandeville worked as a trainer for est, and you could always tell when he'd been to a session, because he would be so high that anyone who didn't share his enthusiasm was a threat. Since I never shared his enthusiasm, I was always a threat. That's what I worried would happen with Max out in the bush. Each of our qualities would be magnified there; mild flaws become major defects when you transport them into the bush.

Like Mandeville, Max wanted to talk about weighty, personal things; I wanted to tell the story of the last time I'd been in Wrangell and had stayed at a place called the Thunderbird Motor Lodge and Laundromat, because I couldn't resist the name.

"Do you let people tell you what to do?" Max asked. I groaned to myself.

That evening we sorted through the equipment at the motel, trying to get rid of some. I explained the plan to Max. "See, we'll land at Chutine

Lake and leave most of the gear. Then we'll fly the raft over to the headwaters of the Barrington and check if we can float it; if we can, we'll kick the raft out of the plane, and hike to it later, then float down the Barrington. I don't know if we can hike up Chutine River to the glaciers for the Barrington and Sheslay, but we'll scope that out. If that doesn't work, we'll see if we can float the Sheslay, and have the pilot leave the kayak down at Taku Lodge. Okay?"

Max didn't say much. He asked a few practical questions—"How far is it from the lake to the headwaters?"—but mostly he was content to let me worry about the plans. "I'm along for the ride," he said with a chuckle.

At six the next morning I took a bleary-eyed peek through the blinds to see what the weather looked like. There were clouds, but it wasn't raining, and it seemed like flying weather. I called out to the strip and talked to Dan Baldwin. "Go back to sleep," he said; "We won't be flying for a while." He was vague about the reason—perhaps he had a hangover, too—but I pulled the blankets over my head.

About nine I got up, feeling less fuzzy, and called again. The weather up the Stikine still wasn't too good, but Baldwin said to come out to the strip by noon and maybe we could go then. Max and I went for breakfast. Once more I was alone with Max at a table, where, while we waited for our food, there was nothing else to do but talk. I wondered aloud how the hiking traverse might go; Max wanted to know if I'd read *Iron John*, the Robert Bly book. I did my best to distract him, to get him on to other topics, or to at least get him to speak more softly, but no luck. We were seated in the center of the café, and amidst the conversations about who had been drunk last night, who was catching how much fish where, and who was having motor problems (car, boat, or plane), Max's claims about having been forced into false ways of thinking, and how he was free of that now, sounded to me as though he were shouting from the top of the table. I pointed out how many large men there were in the café, a reminder that indeed Alaska is different; Max said they didn't realize how trapped they were.

By noon we were at the strip. When we arrived, rain was falling in a flood, the water sheeting off the roof of the Wrangell Air Services trailer. Things didn't seem to be going well. It wasn't just the monsoon, but also that our pilot, Dan Baldwin, was at the hospital. Dan had tried to stop a drum of gasoline from sliding down a steep ramp with his foot that morning and had perhaps broken his ankle. No one yet knew whether he'd be able to fly, or when, and he was the only pilot available for our task.

Meanwhile, I went to find the gear I'd shipped earlier. There had been seven items in the shipment: the raft, two halves of the sea kayak—called a Nautiraid—two metal boxes, and two rubber bags with food and raft gear. But the clerk said only six pieces had showed. We walked around, counting off six pieces each time; the long, skinny bag that held the wooden skeleton of the Nautiraid wasn't there.

The people at the airline assured me lost items usually turned up; when I explained that we needed to leave that day, they said they would fly the missing item to wherever I was. Since this would involve flying a bush plane into the center of a huge, rugged area and finding us in it, when even I didn't know where we would be, I was doubtful.

In a way this simplified my ridiculous plans. The only thing we could do now was fly to Chutine Lake, exit the lake via the Chutine River, and meet up with a plane eight days later somewhere along the Stikine to find out about the missing kayak.

We still had no pilot. Baldwin was in his own holding pattern at the hospital, waiting for X-rays to be taken of his foot. No one seemed to know when he would show up, if he could fly when he did, what would happen if he couldn't, or even if we had a plane to use. It was a circle of waiting: the airline waiting to hear from me about the pilot, me waiting to hear from Wrangell Air, Wrangell Air waiting to hear from the hospital; Wrangell Air waiting to hear from me about the kayak, me waiting to hear from the airline about it, and around again.

I saw the trip crumbling, falling apart. My plans had been pretty poor, certainly, but it was frustrating to watch them come apart. It even occurred to me that I might be on a plane to Iowa soon.

In midafternoon we got the word that Baldwin was coming in from the hospital: no one said whether or not he could fly, just that he was coming. Finally, Dan Baldwin arrived, walking with a lurching limp and carrying crutches. But surprisingly, when he sat down in the office he pronounced himself ready to go, more or less.

"I won't be able to help you lift anything, you know," he said. "You don't have anything heavy, do you? And I may need some help getting in and out. And you might have to help with the foot pedals."

"No problem," I told him, anxious to get going.

"Well, then, let's go," he said, remaining seated on the couch into which he had fallen. In truth he didn't look too good. I had no idea what his usual complexion was, but this day he was white, lightened further by his pale red hair. His lips were white; his skin was white; and even his eyes seemed abnormally white. He looked like someone in a lot of pain.

The airline agent gave me the name of a pilot in British Columbia who would come get the kayak if it showed up and would then bring it to me. I called him on the radiophone and told him the plan, which was to meet us, either with or without kayak, at a creek just downstream from the confluence with the Chutine.

I told Dan Baldwin every step, including when we expected to be out, in case my wife or Max's girlfriend called. He sat patiently while I went over it, with a thoughtful expression that told me he was trying to listen and absorb what I was saying but hadn't heard a word.

At last we could leave. We drove the gear out to the wharf in town, where the 185 was docked. We carried everything down rain-slicked steps and onto the dock, where we crammed it—still too much—into the plane. The flying conditions hadn't improved a bit from what they had been when we'd arrived the day before. Still, we would go.

3   *Fly-In*

Whatever is fitted in any sort to excite the ideas of pain and danger,
that is to say, whatever is in any sort terrible, or is conversant about
terrible objects, or operates in a manner analogous to terror,
is a source of the sublime.
   —Edmund Burke, *On the Sublime and Beautiful*

Dan Baldwin, Max, and I flew across the Eastern Passage, which separates Wrangell Island from the mainland, and over the mouth of the Stikine.
The river looked dark and thick, as though there had been heavy rains upstream—the river was full, nearly splashing over its banks.

It is an inspiring thing, flying up a mountain river in a small plane. It is
also cheating: I have done nothing to earn the inspiration, only rented it.
But cheating is what I must do to get where I want to be. And I love those
flights. The views are tremendous, since I am near enough to the top of the
canyon to see other peaks beyond it, an ocean of white-topped peaks, like
cresting waves. I can see miles up the side canyons, far enough sometimes
to where there is sunshine on the headwater mountains. I pass very near
the walls of the canyon, so close that I can almost feel the water spraying
off one waterfall after another. Flights into the bush also give one a perspective on a type of nothing. No constructions, few sights of humankind,
excluding the plane—it is always a pleasure to see such absence stretching
out, mile upon mile of it.

On my first bush flight, in 1977, I flew in one of the classic bush planes, a
DeHaviland Otter, from the tiny village of Bettles, northwest of Fairbanks,

to Walker Lake, the biggest lake in the Brooks Range. The Otter was brutally loud, could haul an entire river trip of people and gear, and could take off from a short strip and land on both gravel bars and lakes. It was functional and clunky; there wasn't a single graceful thing about it. The roar of the engine made my ears ring for days afterward, so long that I suspected permanent damage, but eventually the ringing faded and I could enjoy the sound of Alaskan silence once again as we floated out of Walker Lake and down the Kobuk River.

Since then I've flown in other bush planes — the Beaver, the Super-Cub, Cessna 185s and 206s rigged as tail-draggers or with floats, and the amphibious Grumman Widgeon — and with some classic bush pilots. This flight up the Stikine prompted memories of those other flights, including one in 1979, a flight that, like this one, was based on a guess. I had convinced the outfitter for whom I worked that a trip on the Ambler River in the Brooks Range would be a good trip, even though I didn't know anyone who had ever floated the river, or whether a plane could land on its upper section. I called an air charter company in Kotzebue to ask about the possibility of landing near the headwaters of the Ambler. They assured me it would be no problem; we would find someplace to land, even if they didn't know where that might be. I wanted to believe it could be done, so I let them convince me it could.

When I left Kotzebue with the pilot, Greg, in a 185 jammed full of gear, we still didn't know if we could land on the Ambler. Back in Kotzebue were a dozen passengers, waiting to fly out later that day to the spot we would pick. As we flew over the flats on the lower Kobuk, then approached the foothills of the Brooks Range, Greg and I shouted to each other above the engine roar. He told me a plan he had, to buy a dirigible, load it with supplies, and spend the summer cruising slowly around the northern interior of Alaska, supplying the remote villages with groceries. He was enthusiastic about the plan; the only drawback, he said, was that the dirigible was so slow that it would take most of the summer to do one tour, but he thought he could compensate by carrying tons of stuff at low cost. His descriptions of the joys of traveling by dirigible were lyrical and made me ready to join him on this slow-motion tour, a blimp on the horizon, moving regally over Alaska.

As we left the valley of the Kobuk and made a left turn up the Ambler, I mentally urged the plane on. The success of the trip depended upon being able to get as high as possible into the mountains that spawned the Ambler. After 120 miles or so up the river, the canyon narrowed dramatically, and we clearly had run out of places to land. The river was flowing too straight and steep to have the twists and turns that make a good gravel bar. But by then we had gone far enough, and if we found a landing spot as soon as we turned and headed back downstream, it would do.

Right away we came to a long stretch of beach on the inside of a left turn in the river. It wasn't very wide, and from the air the gravel looked like quicksand. Greg began to circle above the spot. Again and again he put the plane up on a wing over the spot, estimating the length of it, the size of the rocks, the contour of the beach—if it had too much of a tilt toward the river, it might catapult us into the water; if it had too many dips and valleys, it would invite a nose-first landing. He had told me earlier that the problem was landings, since he would be taking off empty each time and wouldn't need much room then. But of course it would be easier to judge the take-off length—we would be on the ground then—than it was to gauge length from the air. All of this was probably going through his mind as we turned circles, so I didn't interrupt him to point out that I was going to vomit soon.

Then he indicated he would land and wanted to know if this spot was okay. By then, too sick to care, I signalled that landing here, anywhere, would be fine. We started our approach from upstream, Greg keeping his eye on the gravel all the way, waiting until the last moment to decide whether it would work or not. As we dropped lower and lower, the sand became pebbles, then rocks, and nearly boulders to my eye, but since I had no choice, I held on and trusted Greg. He pulled himself up out of his seat to see over the cowling of the engine. In my seat I couldn't see anything but propeller and big stones rushing by my window far too fast. A stall buzzer shrieked, and I was suspended in a dizzying moment, over which I had no control and for which I had no responsibility. When we touched down, a roar erupted from beneath the plane, as rocks were kicked up by the tires and hammered the wings.

We clattered to a stop. Greg turned the engine off, made some witticism, and we climbed out. Climbing out of a bush plane when it has come to rest in the bush is transforming. You wriggle out of the door and stand on the landing gear, and there you are: the bush. The only thing between you and it is this plane, and the plane will soon be gone.

Greg and I scouted the landing strip. It was perfect as far as I was concerned, since it gave us a nice campsite, with a big eddy in which to tie the rafts, and it had a good view west along the southern spine of the Schwatka Mountains, one of the many short ranges that make up the Brooks. We stepped off the length of the strip, one long stride equaling a yard. Greg wanted to have 600 yards of clear gravel for landing. The bar was flat for about 450 yards, but then it angled toward the river for another 100 yards or so. "It's fine," he said anyhow.

We went up and down the bar several times, pushing logs aside and removing the largest rocks. Then Greg was ready to fly back out to begin the shuttle of guides and gear and passengers into our new home. I sat at the low end of the bar, about seventy-five feet beyond what appeared to be the end of the runway, and waited for him to rumble down the beach toward me.

Greg started the 185, the propeller whirring like a noisy toy, and taxied up as far as he could on the bar. He didn't pause even a moment but bounced down the bar, the engine accelerating to an impossibly high pitch. The roar as the plane approached me, the sight of it skittering along the gravel, built to a powerful climax, completed when Greg jerked the wheels free from the ground. He came up fifty yards from me and passed over my head by about twenty-five feet. I fell back on the ground and felt more than saw the metal cross blur above me, all noise and surreal image. I rolled over and watched him fly low over the river a short distance and disappear around a bend. The sound of his motor faded too quickly, and I was left there on a gravel bar, alone with my river bag, one raft, and a box of food, certain that never again in this life would I see Greg or his plane.

———

I tried following the twists and the turns of the river on my map as Dan Baldwin flew on. The tallest peaks of the canyon towered over us. Each peak was a layering of green lower slopes, multicolored streambeds, then gray rock, and a bright white snowfield or glacier on top. We were at eye level with waterfalls, and I could see moose and bear tracks crossing sand

and gravel bars on the river's shore. The side canyons opened up into an Oz, an impossible land of meadows and forests and perfectly clear water; I imagined chesty elks, wolves, bears, unicorns living there undisturbed.

At times I looked down into all of the harsh tones of a deep northern canyon, carved by glaciers; then I looked up, toward hundreds of miles of mountain tops, all white, all of it a testament to wildness. In this land of peaks and snows, there are a dozen or more glaciers feeding the Stikine, some perched high on wind-battered ridges and peaks and others reaching down nearly into the river, as at the Great Glacier, the glacier that John Muir came to on his visit to the Stikine in 1879.

When Dan banked hard to the left, up a tributary that came down through a gray, somber valley, I glanced back and forth from my map to Dan to the river. I tapped Dan and shouted, "What is this?" as I pointed below. He gave me one of those pilot looks before tapping my map, on the wavy line marked "Chutine."

In the canyon, everything changed: the light, since we were now flying north; the color of the land, since the Chutine is a new river, with less vegetation having had a chance to grow on the walls than on those of the Stikine; the canyon itself, because the walls are more sheer and the surrounding peaks even higher, as we were headed into the heart of the Coast Mountains.

After a few seconds of flying up the Chutine, I realized our plans were doomed. An extended hike in this country would take weeks. I might have despaired over this reality, but I couldn't, not in such grand country. There is a type of spectral landscape—bare rock outcroppings in the sea, gravel bars in midriver, glaciers hanging in a high mountain crag—that haunts the mind, intimidates with harshness. This was that kind of landscape.

It was more spectacular than I could have hoped. Much of the valley was bare, stripped clean by glaciers, with glaciers still hanging farther up side valleys, and trees growing only down by the river. We kept going, past the drainage of the Barrington River, past Barrington Mountain, past the confluence with Dirst Creek, and, in the distance, toward a high, gray, sheer face of a mountain wall. We entered an open space above Chutine Lake, surrounded on all sides by huge granite massifs, a shockingly beautiful place.

Dan flew across Chutine Lake to its northern end, then banked and came back to the southwestern edge, where a small island was visible at the base of a wide glacial moraine. Dan dropped the plane down and put us into a long gliding landing on the surface of the lake, which hadn't the least hint of a ripple, and motored the remaining two hundred yards to the beach.

It was as though we had passed through some magic barrier on the flight up the Stikine, some warp between the real world and a fantasy version. We had landed in a Neverland, where all of the natural features had been made more outrageous and beautiful than they could possibly be.

The beach Dan grounded the plane on was brilliant white sand. Looking up from the beach we saw a glacier towering overhead, covering the top of the entire valley that ended in this beach, and glacial till dropped straight down from there, defying gravity as it seemed nearly to be suspended while falling. The lake was a kind of cerulean blue, unlike any color I had ever seen before, as if it had been scraped from the inside of an iceberg and dabbed onto the surface of the lake.

The most demanding form, though, was across the lake from our beach. This was the nearly sheer face of Mt. Chutine, rising 9,633 granitic feet, straight up, the top and bottom in nearly a direct vertical line. From where we stood, the foot of the mountain was only about a mile across the lake, yet its peak was 8,000 feet above us. One ordinarily perceives such height from a distance. The lower slopes of the mountain were gentle, piled with rubble in draws and gullies, and then the angle swept upward, until it became an obelisk of rock, pure granite as far as I could tell. The top was hidden by wispy white clouds that blew past, revealing it only for moments. The mountain was colored along a narrow spectrum of gray, a color one wouldn't ordinarily associate with such drama. The thing was a monument to a type of brutal beauty.

Sid had never stood in the spot where Max and I now were, and he had never seen the mountain from this angle, but he had been in the area. The mountain had been there when Sid had been nearby, and Sid had dug for gold only a few miles behind it, along the Barrington River. It was a connection of sorts—at least, I could imagine it was.

After Max and I unloaded the plane, balancing along the pontoons with the raft, the backpacks, the boxes, paddles, and the half-kayak in its canvas bag, and heaved them on the sand, and after Dan tossed off a few of the standard bush pilot jokes ("Looks like I found you a good place for bears—there ought to be twenty or thirty around." "I'll be back for you . . .

next spring, right?"), we pushed the 185 out, and Dan taxied up the lake. He was off the water in moments, circled to the north, dipped a wing as he came past us, then was gone.

It took some minutes for the sound of his engine to fade, first from hearing and then from our ears as they continued to ring with the memory of the sound. And it was silent. Such silence. A precious moment. You are alone. It is quiet. And as those first moments pass, you become even more alone. And it gets even more quiet. The silence grows, increases, until it turns into the sound of the breeze in the black spruce and reaches a climax in which you become aware of every sound, every movement, every thought and sight. Experience becomes thicker, heavier. But mostly it is quiet, so quiet you become afraid to speak, then you clear your throat just to break the new silence.

We set up a tent back among the thin trees, which were mostly scrubby black spruce, with some cedar and a few cottonwoods. We moved the rest of the gear to a flat spot on the sand, far enough away from the lake waters so that even if the lake rose (a sudden melting of the glacier that fed it, a hurricane springing up out of the blue skies), it wouldn't take our gear from us.

I was fading. I was capable of no more than a quick walk around our new home, back toward the glacier. I couldn't tell how far away the glacier was; something about the color of the ice defeated that kind of measurement. I found the pelvis from a tiny rodent skeleton as we walked. From one angle the pelvis looked like the head of a roaring tiger.

Although I knew trappers had used the lake during the winter, there were no signs of them, but plenty of animal prints. The bear prints were the most obvious, sunk into the soft mud at the edge of the island. Huge pads, the soft round indents for the heel and ball, then the sharp puncture holes of the claws. I found it hard to believe that I was in the neighborhood of something big enough to leave such a mark.

We couldn't get a feel for the place; it was too much to take in at once. We returned to camp, our little toehold on the lake, and I fell into the tent and took notes. As I wrote I listened for the important sounds outside. The soughing of the wind through the trees; the sturdier sound of the wind higher up on the glacier, sweeping down; the crunch of footsteps, which I hoped were those of my partner. There are tiny sounds, too, such as the delicate noise that evergreen needles make when they fall on a dried aspen leaf beneath, a sound that I almost certainly wouldn't notice if I were out of the tent, distracted by sights.

Max came back from his walk—a good noise; it answered the question of whose footsteps those were—and pronounced himself satisfied with our spot. When he came to the door of the tent and looked in, he had a slightly crazed look.

"Hey, man, this is good," he said, grinning madly, which made the dimples in his cheeks cave in. "I'm going to build a rabbit trap."

I was too tired to ask what for. "Great," I said, and zipped the tent's mosquito net closed. In the lingering northern twilight, I read a few pages of Thomas De Quincey's 1821 book, *Confessions of an English Opium-Eater*, which seemed deliciously out of place among the bear prints and glaciers.

I drifted off quickly, not even waking up when Max came in, having burned off some of his energy by whittling. I woke repeatedly during the night, as my body adjusted to sleeping on the ground once more and my mind adjusted to everything else. I was also anxious for morning, when I could throw wide the tent door and see if this place were a dream or real.

4 *Put-In (Chutine Lake)*

Steamboat Syd, on de mighty Yukon!
Steamboat Syd, he's de gamest of dem all!
Steamboat Syd, champion in de pilot-house
He's surely got dem bested in de spring and in de –
 —Song of "Splotus" (Hockie Dennis) from Barrett Willoughby,
  "The Champion Swift-Water Pilot of the North"

There were two things I first learned about Sid: that he was a river man, and that he was "Uncle Sid." Only the former turned out to be true.

——

In the morning I exited the tent into a day that already steamed. The hazy light flattened the surroundings, making them less sharp, but the fantasies of the night before were still there: the massive granite Mt. Chutine, the turquoise lake, the glacier behind us off of which I had heard a distant wind all night, a beautiful sound, an indifferent lament. I burrowed through our supplies, looking for breakfast.

I took photographs while Max slept on, I put gear into piles, jotted notes in my journal, and was lonely. The types of loneliness are infinite, as multiple and varied as the types of love, yet not as well chronicled. Sometimes it is impossible to say what inspires a particular form of loneliness, but wilderness is one thing that does. The feeling of loneliness that comes over me in a wild place is a barometer of wilderness, for only true wilderness inspires it.

I became aware of the loneliness of wilderness after my first season in Alaska, when the manic Bo Mandeville and I traveled with friends of his from Fairbanks down to the Kenai Peninsula, where we helped build a log cabin, and back up to Anchorage, and finally to Denali Park. While hiking at the foot of Denali, I stopped to take a leak and looked out over a valley woven in fall colors, and despair filled me. It was a glorious sight, but it made me desperately unhappy—despair at my inability to deal with this valley. I stared out over the tundra, and it just seemed too much: too much beauty, too much wild-ness, too big for me. How strange that felt, to be overwhelmed by wilderness.

Overwhelmed isn't the only way I felt in Denali, but it is one of the first emotions I have when in a true spot, and it becomes a test: do I feel threatened? Yes? Then I am in a wilderness, I have arrived, and now I can go on to the next sensation.

As I puttered about on the beach, I occasionally straightened up and looked around—this look, too, comes from being in a wild place. I begin to look at one thing, and my gaze is pulled along the horizon by the other things to see, by the absence of the familiar: buildings, structures, cars, people. Each time I scanned the surroundings it was a mild shock, the sight of all this, all this, all this . . . I couldn't quite say what it was. The only word was "nothing," all of this nothing, but of course that wouldn't do, because nothing is exactly what it wasn't. It was a plenitude, of forms and shapes and colors.

In another hour Max stumbled out of the tent. I looked at him, he looked at me, each of us shocked to find ourselves alone together. Slowly he turned a circle. "Holy cow," he said, looking up. "What a place." He giggled.

On that first morning we stretched out on the blond beach at Chutine Lake. We talked about river guides, about the ones I had known and the ones Max had met on his travels. I tried to explain guiding to him and got out Edward Abbey's book *Down the River* and read his description: "These boatmen. These jet-set river guides. . . . Bright, handsome, talented young men with many skills, equally adept at river running, cooking, rock climbing, glacier trekking, search and rescue, fishing, hunting, skiing, guitar, harmonica, song. True outdoorsmen, who not only know but also love the out-of-doors. And indeed, how could you know it unless you loved it? As on any commercial river trip, the boatmen—and often, these days, the boatwomen—are the best part of the trip."

Then Max made a terrible mistake: "So, how'd you get into guiding?" he asked, and I told him the story . . .

———

In the spring of 1973 I was a sophomore at Berkeley. The spring before, the city had been howling with protests and riots, following the U.S. mining of Haiphong Harbor in Vietnam. For a week I'd attended the spectacle, the daytime rallies of thousands and the nighttime skirmishes through Berkeley's leafy streets. I was gassed, clubbed, shot by rubber bullets; I passed out leaflets, chanted silly slogans, slept hardly at all. I ran wild in the streets, never quite sure whether I was a spectator or participant. I listened for the sound of squad cars and angry shouts and learned how to cope with pepper gas. That was the spring when an antiwar march through campus could seem from the middle, where I stood, endless in either direction.

But that was the year before, and now I was bored. I envied a friend who had dropped out of San Francisco State to wander south to Mexico and hitchhike around the United States. I had tried every drug that had passed my way. I had a six-inch feather earring, a long braid of hair, and a beard confined to two inches of my chin. I was thoroughly nineteen.

If I was bored with my nineteen-year-old life, I loved the school. Moses Hall, which held the Philosophy Library, was shrouded by dogwoods and Japanese maples, so that we philosophy students could sit in the appropriate philosophical gloom even on the brightest days. And the first time I saw Doe Library was on a September night, when the curved steps leading to the entrance were wrapped in fog and seemed to ascend toward Athens itself: pillars rising out of the fog, and inside, matching marble staircases leading to room after room of books—obscure books, old books, great books, complicated books, slim books.

For a time I had a campus job at the Graduate School of Public Policy, which provided me with a pass to the stacks in Doe, a privilege I never would have earned on my own. I spent my lunch time wandering among the stacks, checking out (in the name of some innocent professor of public policy) Alfred Jarry's *Pere Ubu,* an early edition of Baudelaire's *Flowers of Evil,* all the Kerouac, and any other Beat writing I came across.

I even enjoyed my professors, who, in the devotion they had given to some arcane subject, seemed more flamboyant and wild than any of the

Berkeley street poets wearing motorcycle boots and scarves, reading their ragged poetry in the coffeehouses along Telegraph Avenue. Even so, I quit school after the winter quarter in 1973 and went looking for work.

On a bulletin board at the university I found what I was looking for: a job washing dishes at a seedy restaurant on the lower end of University Avenue, where prostitutes hung out and hitchhikers caught rides onto Highway 80. The restaurant was as dark as a place could be and still claim to have lights; the owner was surly and from the Middle East somewhere, and he thought I was twenty-one, so I would have been able to drink in the bar if I had wanted to.

I didn't take the job, so I'll never know what lessons I might have learned from the nether end of University Avenue. While looking at the notices on the bulletin board, I saw one that, as I recall, went like this:

RIVER GUIDES
Whitewater river guides needed. Applicants should be experienced and in excellent physical condition.

Although I didn't know what a river guide was, I called the number, set up a meeting with the outfitter who was hiring, and went, carefully stashing my earring in the glove box of my VW.

Somewhere Sartre claims the irreducible fact of human existence to be that, despite the infinite ways in which one can live, ultimately one's life is just a single narrative. I was poised between several stories—the one that began at dishwasher, or the one starting at river guide. One life would have gone west on University Avenue to the corner of University and San Pablo; the other headed north and east to the Sierra and Siskiyous and Cascades and Sawtooths and Brooks Range.

———

The sun was intense on our beach. In keeping with the insane variety surrounding us, there were other weathers nearby: the glacier behind us owned a wind, a constant muted roar that swept off the glacier and into the trees, dying there; even more bizarre, across the lake, was the sight of Mt. Chutine, whose granite face was slashed by shadows crossing it as the sun moved around it but whose top was utterly obscured in dark, drifting clouds. Then, as the clouds passed and lifted, they revealed to us that it was snowing up there. It was at least 85 degrees where we were, so warm that we were as stripped down as the mosquitoes would permit, yet within hailing distance, almost, there was snow, heavy snow from the looks of it.

I had abandoned all previous plans. Since we were here, we would explore: paddle the raft to the head of the lake, the north end, and maybe traverse to the headwaters of the Barrington River, to explore up that way. From our beachfront sitting spot, we could see the smooth slopes of the glacier (a round dome curving above the distant ridges to the north like a misplaced sports stadium) that gave the Barrington its initial water, and we thought we could hike up the drainage of the feeder creek—Chutine Creek—or along the granite footings of Mt. Chutine toward that glacier, then cross it and descend into the valley of the Barrington. No problem.

Then we unrolled the raft.

It looked fragile and old, lying there flat in the sand. Like dogs, rafts age at a different rate than humans. Each raft year is equivalent to about five human years. I had bought this one in 1977, for a trip down the Grand Canyon, so it was seventy raft-years old. Patches dotted it from scrapes on rivers in Alaska, in the Grand Canyon and in-between, and the D-rings (metal rings in a round-with-one-side flattened shape: "D") were starting to separate in places from the raft's material. The sight of the raft lying there—gray, crumpled, wrinkled, our only transport out of this wilderness —was not inspiring. I watched Max as we rolled out the raft. He frowned. "This is it?" he asked, failing to keep the dismay out of his voice. "How old is it?"

"Oh, I don't know," I said, searching for a euphemism. "It's been around."

We pumped the raft, and it looked a little more lively as each compartment came taut. It is about fourteen feet long and six feet wide, and the tubes are twenty-four inches in diameter. There are four compartments around the edges and two thwarts running across. In comparison to modern rafts, with self-bailing floors and special features, my raft was pathetic, sad, an anachronism, the rafting equivalent of bell-bottoms.

I called it the *Oyster Dunny*. In the late '70s, a woman and her son lived next door to the warehouse in Angels Camp where we kept the river equipment we used on the late Stanislaus River (flooded, damned by a dam). I was preparing the gear for another rafting season and dropped by their house on Easter Sunday. The boy had drawn an Easter card for his mother, with a large rabbit and several mixed-up greetings, so the card read,

Hone sweat hone,
love, the Oyster Dunny.

"Oyster Dunny" sounded like a name for a watercraft in Alice in Wonderland, and I claimed it for my own.

After we pumped up the *Dunny*, we piled the things we were leaving behind on the beach and covered them with a canvas tarp, then loaded the backpacks and food and river bags into the back of the raft and pushed off.

That first moment in a boat, any boat, is a pleasure: the sensation of floating, of depending on aqueous rather than terrestrial support, the cool air currents off the water, the changed perspective now that one is surrounded by water. We stroked toward the middle of the lake, heading for the eastern shore at the foot of Mt. Chutine. Out in the middle we stopped for a moment and lay back against our gear, toasting in the sun, to watch the snow fly and winds whip on the top of the mountain.

"Jesus, I'm roasting," said Max.

"What do you think, sixty degrees colder up there?" I wondered.

"At least," returned Max, looking up, then squinting back down at the horizon line above the lake. "This sure is humbling land." I nodded. "Humbling" was a good word for it.

Our sense of isolation was perfect as we basked in the middle of the lake. It was as though no humans had ever been there, though that wasn't so. We took up our paddles and continued, marveling at the blue-turquoise beneath us and the uniformity of its color. The top inch or two of the lake surface was transparent, but below that, the color was a solid block that my eye couldn't penetrate.

It took about an hour to paddle to the other side of the lake, a shore that was a sheet of granite disappearing straight down into the lake. No shoreline, just plunging wall. We paddled along the base of the mountain, reaching out constantly to touch it, until, a hundred yards from the beach that stretched along the north end of the lake, we saw the only sign of human construction: a few sticks leaning against each other to make a fish-drying rack. I had heard that there was a Tahltan Indian by the name of Billy who trapped here in winter, and this must have been his camp.

We landed the raft on the beach and claimed it in the name of us. After hauling our packs and a few river bags out of the raft, we lifted it up by the D-rings and walked it onto level ground. We both noticed that the raft had gotten spongy on the paddle across the lake.

"Is it always like that?" Max asked.

"No," I said reassuringly. "It's just the cold water making the air inside contract." Surely, I thought, Max should recognize the principle of contraction and expansion—although the raft did seem to be surprisingly floppy. I tried to remember the last time I'd used it and whether it had leaked, but I couldn't. I knew I should have checked it out before leaving Maine; that, like so many other things I should have done, I hadn't.

After tying the *Oyster Dunny*, we plotted our next move. Our choices were simple: backpack up Chutine Creek to the headwaters of the Barrington. Or, nap in the sand.

Despite the fact that it looked to be a good ten miles to the glacier, and by now we were aware of how hard walking in this country would be, we agreed it had to be done—or at least attempted. A curious lassitude had settled over me in the morning, and I couldn't lift it. It came from wilderness and from feeling incompetent, incompetent for not having predicted the way things would be out here. I am not a guide anymore, I reminded myself, as I trudged along. I should have thought this through better; Sid would have figured it out, Sid would have known what to do . . .

———

Surprisingly, I was hired as a guide, the youngest one in that outfitter's crew, in spite of my attempts to compose a whitewater résumé in the middle of my interview ("Oh sure, I've been on lots of rivers."). I suppose one reason was that in the early '70s, commercial whitewater rafting in California was new, and there were very few experienced river guides—people without experience had to be hired, truth-stretchers or not.

New guides were always trained in the spring, when the rivers of the Sierra Nevada are high and icy cold, when the small towns near the rivers are still sleepy, when the wildflowers in the open grassy fields explode on the hillsides, especially in the oak-and-pine canyons. If I hadn't known what whitewater rafting was before I went for my interview, this is what it became for me: big blue waves, cold water, quiet towns, wildflowers and canyons.

Late in March of 1973 the eight guides—four trainees, two veterans, and the two outfitters we worked for—began running the rivers. The eight of us didn't have much else in common, but we shared a naked enjoyment of this experience, of the water and the canyon, and being there while everybody else in the world was stuck doing what he or she had always done. Images of that week of training were vivid for years: the eight of us huddling under the porch awning of an abandoned cabin by the Stanislaus, trying to sleep out of the rain; getting stoned in the old, green, ex–Forest Service bus that the outfitters used to shuttle equipment and passengers; my feeling that this river business was tame, until I was flipped off the back of the raft into the freezing water during one of the first few rapids on the Stanislaus.

Raft guiding, like other forms of guiding, involves compromises. When guiding, the guide is not on his or her own; the guide has obligations to the paying customers and isn't free to behave as he otherwise would. A hunting guide is different from a hunter; a mountain guide is different from a mountaineer. Turning a skier into a ski guide converts her into a slightly diminished thing. The guide gives up a little piece of his independence in making the conversion, gives up a tiny bit of himself as well.

The essence of all forms of guiding is pretty simple, hence the appeal in a postmodern world. In the case of commercial rafting, people pay to be taken out onto a river and protected from the river, the shore, starvation, boredom. Sometimes during the season we felt as though we were running rides at Disneyland, and sometimes we were what we really were: guides, without whom the passengers would be lost. Most raft guides are not naturalists—though some are—or experts at anything but getting a raft down a river and dealing with the camping on shore. Guides don't have to be good shots with a rifle, experts in backwoods lore, tall, rugged, or brave—though some are. Rafting isn't particularly dangerous, either, but it can be. I've been around broken legs, broken backs, broken noses; I've done helicopter evacuations, seen people disappear beneath rapids for far too long, been on a river when dead bodies were afloat both up- and downstream.

In that first season, most of my trips were on the Stanislaus, and most of the trips were on weekends, with a night spent at a big bend in the river, across from a limestone cliff known as Shark's Mouth. We made the meals here and were entertaining in various ways, usually by telling stories of different rivers and trips, inflating our already inflated self-images.

The other river we worked was the Tuolumne. The Tuolumne at the time was the river guide's El Capitan, the pinnacle of the profession, though Grand Canyon guides would dispute this. It was the most challenging river we ran then and the most tightly regulated, so you were an elite guide if you were a Tuolumne guide, and the river was yours—it was too hard, too dangerous for private boaters, so we'd rarely see anyone else on the river during the two- or three-day trips we ran. In the spring the water was high and fast, and in the summer the river became a boulder garden. By late summer the canyon sizzled, too, so that the cold water felt good instead of just cold, and wearing nothing but a pair of shorts and rotten tennis shoes from dawn until we flopped down in our bags at night felt right.

In the heart of the summer, we thought about such things as the sensation of sand squished between toes, or the adrenaline rush of lining up for the shot at Clavey Falls, or the lull of rocking on a hot raft in the sun, or the sight of the canyon's orange and green shadows on the river's surface, and not of much else. We became something other than what we had been in our earlier lives—pieces of the canyon, creatures who fit in there, who belonged there.

Eventually I guided on most of the runnable rivers in northern California, on the Rogue and Owyhee in Oregon, on the Middle Fork and Main in Idaho, on the Green in Utah, and once on the Colorado through Grand Canyon. In 1977 I went to Alaska for the first time. It was the first of seven consecutive summers when I would be in the Brooks Range to guide, and it may have been on the 1977 trip that I discovered there was such a person as "Uncle Sid."

I would have been visiting my grandmother on Whidbey Island, in Oak Harbor, the same town the Barringtons were from. My grandmother was born on Whidbey and lived for most of her life at the high end of a sloping prairie that ended in the harbor. The slope was part of the original donation claim of 160 acres made to Ulrich Freund, my great-great-great-great-uncle, one of the three men who first settled the midsection of the island in 1848.

I don't remember it, but I can imagine it: my grandmother would have been standing next to me at the kitchen table, looking out the big windows onto the field of Queen Anne's lace, and on Oak Harbor below, a scene she had viewed from that spot for almost eighty years. She was a proud, rather proper woman, and her status as grandmother required that others carry the conversational burden. She rarely asked me any questions, not until I had been at her house for a day or two and had emptied my store of insipid observations: "Windy out today!" I would shout toward her good ear. "Getting dark!" I would shout a few hours later.

I can hear how it might have been, my grandmother saying after a few days of my visit, "You know, Uncle Sid was a river man, too . . ."

———

Max and I walked across the alluvial fan at the mouth of Chutine Creek. After a short hike, we came to the bottom of granite sheets that were slipping off the sides of Mt. Chutine. Walking was easy over the smooth granite, and it gave us a view of what was next. We could see that the easy walking was going to peter out soon, where the granite dropped into the creek valley. We stripped down to fanny packs and a small knapsack with climbing gear. We left our big packs tied in a tree.

Scrambling higher up the granite, we were able to move effortlessly over the rock, and it was lovely. With each step upward, the views expanded, as though the horizon were being peeled back for us. On the steepest places, on hands and knees on the granite, I found myself reading the rock, as though it were a text, or as though I were crawling over a huge, glorious canvas.

A porcupine waddled toward us along the granite. Like us, he had figured out that the walking was much better up here; when he took note of us, though, he turned and wiggled off into the brush downhill. Before he disappeared, we could see that the back of his pelt was stripped bare—something had taken a swipe out of him.

We headed more or less north on the sloping sheets of granite, toward the Barrington, until we came to the end of the granite and dropped toward Chutine Creek: a ravine choked with cedars and devil's club, that aptly named weed that grows in wet areas in the Northwest and has spikes all along its leaves and stalk (even on its roots, I imagine). Lower now, we were in a landscape where visibility was reduced to the trees directly in front of us, to either side, and behind. There were game trails winding through the underbrush, but the problem with game trails is that they rarely go where you want.

We looked ahead of us, we looked behind, we looked at each other. "How far do you think we've come?" I asked.

"Not far," Max said, looking back toward the lake. "A mile?"

"Maybe. Now's the hard part, eh? Nine miles of bushwhacking."

We looked north, in the direction of those nine miles. We squinted and stood; squinted, and stayed. There is a type of squinting that means, I am not going that way. We had that squint on. If one of us had taken a step forward, north, then we would have gone, but instead we just looked. Independently we were calculating the value of those nine miles: we had a nice spot back at the lake, and after we'd walked nine miles north, we'd have to walk ten miles south, and for what? What were we doing it for? So that we could say we'd seen the headwaters of the Barrington?

Miserable sluggards, we turned back, opting, we told ourselves, for exploring more of the lake. As we retreated along the granite, Max muttered something about "learning our limits," and I was silently grateful to the airline for having saved us from my bad ideas.

Back at the lake Max got ambitious and decided to try a bath. Coming fresh off of glaciers, the lake water was brutally cold, but in the midday heat—mid eighties or so—it didn't feel so bad when I put my finger in up to the first knuckle. Max stripped down and plunged in, then plunged right back out.

"Christ!" he shouted as he came roaring out of the water, legs pumping.

He still seemed to be in pain, even after he was out. "Cold?" I asked, sitting in the hot sand.

"Oh shit, oh man," Max groaned.

He soaped himself up a little, then tried to rinse without actually touching the lake water again, but he had to step into it a few inches to gather water, only to hop out a second later.

We lazed about in the sun, trying various prophylactics for the bugs. I draped a large bandana over my head, with a baseball cap pulled down tight over it, so that I looked like a low-rent Lawrence of Arabia. Max told the story of how the inhabitants of Walter Raleigh's Lost Colony of North Carolina were driven mad by mosquitoes.

It was July fourth. We cooked a dinner of freeze-dried something and continued talking. For two men who had known each other only a few days, we certainly had a lot to talk about. We talked about loving children, and what it means to be a man, and whether or not it is better to serve the community or yourself. We didn't think alike about anything.

"I wonder what my wife's doing," I mused.

"Probably trying to stay off her broken tailbone," Max replied reasonably, and I pulled my hat down over my eyes.

I went for a walk after dinner, out to an odd knob in the alluvial fan behind camp. From there I could see a half-dozen waterfalls, Owens Peak to the west, and part of the way up a glacial drain that swept into Chutine Creek, colored in somber hues, ocher and grays, plus the turquoise and white of the creek. To the north was the clogged valley of Chutine Creek, and beyond, the knoll of the glaciers we had tried—barely—to reach. To the east were the granite flanks of Mt. Chutine and the peak itself, soaring straight up. Everywhere were testaments to glaciers, including the glaciers themselves reaching down to the lake like so many white, bony fingers.

Outrageous. That was the word that throbbed in my head as I looked. Everything was too large, and out of proportion. There were scrubby little bushes at my feet and a sheer-walled river canyon with a major roaring torrent pouring through it only 250 yards away. As Max had said earlier, "humbling land."

I felt tiny. Tiny is not bad; tiny is the way you are supposed to feel at such moments. But I also felt trapped. I was in the most unrestricted place I could possibly be, and it was as though I were in a stalled elevator. This was all wrong. I was crushed, smaller than tiny. I needed to be someplace else but couldn't be.

Back at camp I told Max about it. He nodded, poking a stick into the fire. "You aren't in control of this," he said.

"In control of what?"

"This," he said, lifting his arms up to the Chutine basin. "You can't control it, and that freaks you out."

The subject of Control had been one of our themes so far, a dangerous one since we disagreed completely. I claimed that people had plenty of control over their lives, while Max said this was an illusion. We would argue on and on, providing examples to support our positions, occasionally contradicting ourselves. It would have been better to agree sometimes with my partner, but I couldn't help it, I couldn't let him go unchallenged.

This time he was probably right. It bothered me that I had so little control of the situation. For the moment I was stuck here; my wife, who may or may not have needed me, was thousands of miles away, and there wasn't much I could do about it.

Into the Independence night we went, tossing stones, telling tales, talking about power and control. Max took two pieces of quartz and rubbed them together, creating a spark that seemed to come from inside the rocks: the "piezoelectric effect," he called it. The sky around us dimmed only gradually. At midnight it was still a soft blue, and I stuck the ends of a few long pieces of wood into the fire. When the sticks flamed, I pulled them out of the fire and whirled them. The flames quickly went out, leaving only the embers at the end of the sticks, glowing redder as I whipped the sticks around. I sang the "Star-Spangled Banner" and made the embers trace patterns in the semidarkness, and at "the home of the brave," I tossed the sticks into the lake with a whoop and watched them expire in a sizzle. Max clapped, and I realized it was the wrong place, the wrong time: we were in Canada, and it was now July fifth.

The massifs around the lake were just silhouettes, shadows etched in the stars. Starlight glimmered a bit off the surface of the lake, and the only sounds were the crackling of the fire and the steady ones: the rumble of the creek and the thrumming sigh of a waterfall, somewhere.

———

I was hooked, even though he wasn't my uncle. He was the son of Edward Barrington, a red-headed sea captain who had come around Cape Horn in 1852 on a schooner from Nova Scotia. Barrington landed in San Francisco, then headed north a few years later to the new territory of Washington and eventually to Whidbey Island and Oak Harbor. He promptly made a name for himself, first by taking an Indian wife, then by defending the local Skagit Indians from an attack by the more aggressive Haida Indians. This he did by taking the skull from a native burial canoe and greeting the marauders with war whoops and howls. Only the Devil would take such liberties with the dead.

After abandoning his native wife, Barrington married Christina McCrohan, an Australian immigrant twenty-eight years younger than him, and sired a herd of boys—Edward Jr., Harry, Yorke, Sidney, and Hill—and a daughter, Sibella.

Edward Senior, the red-headed demon, hoped his sons would be doctors; most of all he hoped they would not be sailors. His luck with directing the lives of his sons was about average: only one son, Hill, actually made it to medical school but quit after a year, while another, Yorke, became a pharmacist and died from a brain aneurysm on the streets of Seattle. In 1892 Sid was seventeen and on the waterfront in Seattle, working as a mate on ferryboats, and by 1896 he was a captain with coastwise navigation papers.

The Klondike gold strike was made in that year, but because of the Yukon winters, word didn't get out until June of 1897. There are several versions of Sid and his brother Edward's subsequent arrival in Alaska. One version has it that when news of the Klondike went out with a roar, he and Ed were already there, "at some Alaskan port" in late June of 1897, where he saw a southbound ship that had "a couple of tons of gold on board from the Klondike," and they immediately left for the Klondike. In another version, Sid and Ed left for Alaska the day after that ship docked in Seattle. They got to Dyea on the Inside Passage, then traveled over the Chilkoot Pass, a thirty-mile trail, much of it straight up. Years later, Sid remembered that while on the Chilkoot, "I often looked back at the hundreds of men with packs, and wondered what the hell we were all doing it for."

Upon arriving in Dawson, they immediately set out on a stampede up the Klondike River to prospect sixty or eighty miles into the interior, staking claims as they went. By 1898 Sid and Ed had a claim on Bonanza Creek, a tributary of the Klondike. In a letter Ed sent home to Oak Harbor during the season, he says that his and Sid's claims were worth about $55,000 and that in the fall they would sell out both.

The gold mining seems to have been just an excuse to get into the Klondike, because once there, the brothers were distracted by their real love: boats and water. In early 1898, Ed had arranged for the purchase of a steamer, the *Aquila*, and in February he sailed for Alaska with it. He had planned to take the *Aquila* over the Chilkoot Pass (a trip which several vessels made in pieces), but found this plan impossible, so he had the steamer sent around to St. Michael at the mouth of the Yukon, to come upriver and meet him in Dawson, a trip of nearly two thousand miles just on the river portion. While waiting for the *Aquila*, Ed and two partners arranged to lease another steamer, the *Willie Irving* ("the most ramshackle-looking little stern-wheeler that ever grounded on a river bar," according to Sid), and ran passengers upstream from Dawson to Whitehorse Rapids, through Five Fingers Rapid and Lake Laberge.

Ed says, in a letter to his mother on June 25, 1898, "I have made three trips with this old box [probably the *Willie Irving*] I am running for the AC Co. [the Alaska Commercial Company] I am running her just to learn the channel . . . I am saving to buy one half of her or all of her. I am half crazy worrying about the Aquila I am loosing just $1000 a day by her not being here this old box I am on now has made $21,600 in the 3 trips i have run here 13 days work she can only go up stream 2 miles an hour so if the aquila will get here she will make a good clean up if I can only get in 30 days work." Despite being limited to "this old box," at the end of the season, Sid said, the *Willie Irving* had cleared $127,000.

In the summer of 1898, typhoid swept through Dawson. Ed writes, "Chris [Fischer, a Whidbey Island neighbor] has been very sick but was better when I left was up and around he had the diarea. Every one in Dawson has it and I think he was on the verge of having the scurvy . . . things are terrible in Dawson at present." On a trip upriver in July, Ed fell ill with typhoid. He returned in the *Willie Irving* to Dawson, where Sid took over operation of the *Irving*. Ed was nursed for three weeks by his brother Hill, who had joined Ed and Sid that summer, but on August 29 he died.

Sid and Hill packed up Ed's remains, took them upstream on the *Willie Irving*, across the lakes, and carried them over the Dyea trail to put aboard the *City of Seattle*. The telegram sent to Yorke Barrington in Seattle on September sixteenth said simply, "Boys will be home on City Seattle with remains Ed Barrington." At the bottom of the telegram a cheery advertisement reminded them, "Time is your competitor!" After sixteen days they arrived in Oak Harbor and buried Ed in the family plot overlooking the harbor.

After the death of Ed, Sid's career as the "Champion Swift-Water Pilot of the North" truly began, a career that became famous in its modest way only because Sid had his own biographer, an American writer of romances, adventures, and travel of the '20s and '30s named Barrett Willoughby. Somehow Willoughby hooked up with Sid, and he became the subject of a number of her works. He is featured in the nonfiction *Gentlemen Unafraid* (a collection of tales about Alaskan pioneers) and *Sitka, Portal of Romance* and is the basis for the fictionalized character Revelry Bourne in her novel *River House*.

Willoughby's fascination with Sid is obvious. In *Gentlemen Unafraid*, she describes Sid as "lean and keen-eyed, a lightning thinker, and swift as a panther in action." And Revelry Bourne in *River House* positively glows: "He sauntered forward, attractively negligent in white flannels and a pullover sweater, the sun on his dark gold hair. . . . [He] was a lean, long-limbed fellow at the high noon of his youth . . . there was about him something unhurried and sure and powerful, like the mobile strength of rivers that are swift and deep."

The setting for the chapter in *Gentlemen Unafraid* is the deck of one of Sid's boats in the late '30s, during a trip up the Stikine. Willoughby records Sid reflecting on the tales of his youth, interspersed with her own commentary and testimonials from an unnamed "mate" and another "pioneer of the north." Unfortunately, the stories that Willoughby has Sid tell are so improbable, it is hard to take them seriously; it's even harder to separate the kernel of truth from the husk of tall tales.

According to Willoughby, Sid—having returned to Dawson—sold the *Willie Irving* after Ed's death and took the $50,000 profit downstream with him as a passenger on another steamboat. Says Sid, "We hadn't gone more than two bends and a look before he [the pilot] ran her high and dry on a gravel bar. The Captain was so disgusted he sent the pilot ashore. When we got the steamer off he asked me to take her down to St. Michael, which was about fifteen hundred miles west. I was really glad to do it because being a passenger gets monotonous." Sid, claims Willoughby, then piloted the steamboat fifteen hundred miles down the Yukon to St. Michael where he bought an old steamer, which he had barged to Nome.

Nome during the Alaskan gold rush was a small city, with its own phone system and several newspapers. It also had several gambling houses, including Tex Rickard's place, the Northern. Rickard had been a Texas Ranger who went to Dawson for gold, then opened up gambling and dance halls instead, and eventually managed prizefights in Madison Square Garden.

Willoughby tells the story of what happened the night Sid arrived with his steamer: Sid sat down at a faro table in the Northern, owning the little steamer and $32,000 in cash, and by morning had lost both.

Tex loaned Sid enough to get out of Nome and back to Oak Harbor. After his season of adventure and profit in the Yukon, he arrived home busted. He claimed it didn't bother him, but this, too, is hard to imagine. As an iron winter gripped the north, Sid rested around the family hearth. I don't know what else he did that winter, but the next season, 1899, he returned to the Yukon—this time not as a miner but as the youngest riverboat pilot on the Yukon.

———

In the morning the air outside the tent was cool and pleasant, but I could feel how tight my face was from old mosquito bites. The bridge of my nose had swelled so much that my head felt like a balloon about to burst. I had to drench myself in bug dope, then wear my bandana tucked down into my collar and over my head, with a long-sleeved shirt buttoned tight, while sitting in the smoke from a cooking fire in the middle of the sun-savaged beach.

I made myself instant everything—oatmeal and coffee—then sat in the sand taking notes through two cups of coffee, swatting bugs with my free hand at the same time. Insects kept landing in my coffee and expiring in the heat. I strained them out through tightly clenched teeth.

I wondered what Sid would think of Max and me, at Chutine Lake for no good reason. Why bother going if you're not getting paid? might be the question Sid would ask, although perhaps he knew. Anyone with an undamaged soul can appreciate the aesthetics of wilderness: a creek all alone in a forest, say, or a stand of trees ascending a ridge; the experience of the silences as well as the sounds. The silence is rare, the sounds complicated, particularly those made by rivers and rapids. One has to shout over the noise of a rapid, but one can also whisper beneath that roar and be heard.

Others have pointed out that all of your senses are engaged when you are in a wild place. Every sense is working, every sense has something to do. Those other senses are engaged, too—the spiritual, the metaphysical. And as those senses of mine engage, it makes me larger, because I am in an intimate relationship with the wildness. But while it enlarges me, it—paradoxically—diminishes me, because I am lost in it, a minor to its major. To be humbled yet lifted up at the same time seems like a good reason to seek out wild places.

Sid's reasons for spending his working life on rivers were practical. I know he loved rivers, but they were also his business. It was once a business to me, too, an occupation, although my motivation for guiding was mostly the thrill of it, the escape from the ordinary. At times I was also burdened by an ambivalence about it, and I wondered if Sid ever felt this way. Like most river guides, I worked in spring and summer, sometimes as late as mid October in California. After that, I had nothing at all to do with guides or guiding. By the time I left at the end of the season, I was thoroughly sick of guiding and sure I wasn't coming back the next season. When I was guiding, I would think longingly of the things I could get in the city: a newspaper, a good cup of morning coffee at a breakfast place on College Avenue in Oakland, someone to serve me a meal, sleeping in a bed rather than on the ground, the time to read a book. While guiding, I thought I should be doing practical things; when I was doing practical things, such as being in college, I thought I should be on a river. I'd always been frustrated by this divided mind, wondering if it meant I was a river dilettante. I was—a dilettante who always returned.

Like me, Sid worked a half-year river season. In the winters he returned to Seattle or Oak Harbor and gambled. I wondered whether, when he left Wrangell in September, he was tired of the whole thing and couldn't wait to get back to the city, or whether he left with regret, left only because the river would soon be impossible to run.

At the end of the second cup of coffee, I came back to Sid and what he might think of us, this July day almost a hundred years after he'd left for the Yukon—Would he approve? Or would he lower his brow, squint, and say, "Why? What for?" I couldn't imagine him doing this, going off into the woods, to a river, for reasons as slight as mine were. He might call it indulgent, capricious, faux adventuring—words he'd probably never use. But did this mean Max and I were being indulgent, capricious, having a faux adventure by being here?

Sweating in the sun, I became too uncomfortable to continue these ruminations. Besides, it was time to get moving. Max was up, rubbing the sleep from his eyes. Max is one of those people who wake up slowly, who might or might not respond to a joke first thing, and who usually look disheveled, incoherent, and mildly hostile in the morning. I wouldn't have attempted a witticism at his expense during his first waking hour.

"Good morning," I said perkily.

"Yeah," muttered Max, scratching his thinning hair. I tried to think of some other agreeable thing to say. Most of our conversations so far had been either practical or arguments. It would have been nice to come up with some friendly, facile comment, but I couldn't find the words, and the strain of trying to find them made them even more distant.

We had decided to explore other parts of the lake, then leave the next morning for the lower part of the lake and the river. Across Chutine Creek from us, on the northwest corner of the lake, was a red knoll that formed a wedge between a glacial outlet cutting across its north side and Chutine Creek flowing past its east edge. The color was odd, since it was the only red rock in the whole valley, and it was solidly red, like a drunk's nose. There were few trees on it; we thought we could probably get a decent view up the valley of the Chutine from there, and we would see whether we had been fools or prescient not to pursue our hike over to the headwaters of the Sheslay.

We grabbed binoculars and a few things to eat and made sure that camp was secure. We pumped up the *Oyster Dunny* again, since it had become depressingly flat overnight, and hopped in for a quick paddle across the lake. There we scooted into an eddy, shaded by one tree to which we tied the raft, trying to avoid the sharp rocks on shore that could have punctured the *Dunny*. We scrambled up past this shale and walked on the smooth red stone.

The humps on the way up the knob were smooth, like the flesh of a huge lizard, and each level seemed to be tilted at an agreeable walking angle, switching back and forth. After a while we were forced to climb more steeply. We nearly stepped on a single tern's egg, set with care in a crease in an exposed section of the rock, so it wouldn't roll off.

We passed from the knoll across a narrow earth bridge to the main canyon wall of schist. We labored upward, sliding down in a shower of rock shards. There wasn't much to hold onto, and no sign of the ascent leveling off. From this elevated perch we could see far up Chutine Creek. The terrain up there was no different from what we'd encountered the day before: dense forest until it ended at the glacier of the Barrington. It would have been a difficult hike, although that didn't keep me from embarrassment that we hadn't tried a little harder.

I looked over the edge of the slope we were on and down into the canyon of the unnamed glacial river. Glacial water doesn't carry much with it in the way of seeds or soil: it is mostly crushed rock and ice and very cold water, so the canyons that the water forms are barren, like this one, which was a smooth V with black-and-tan sides, nothing on shore but gravel and a few clumps of fireweed, that lovely dark pink invader, which grows where fire has been.

The water rushed past without pause or cease, without any calm anywhere—these glacial rivers don't believe in eddies. The creek was a flood of water that was about as pure as water can be; it was water that flowed unimpeded, and no one wanted to use it, or dam it, or divert it, or exploit it, and in the eyes of an American living in the late twentieth century, there was something wonderful about the sight of water that is pure excess, flowing off into a lake where it won't be captured by anyone for anything.

After struggling upward for a little longer, we halted. We were on the edge of a magnificent valley; there wasn't another soul around in any direction, unless I counted Max, and I guessed I would have to; I had rarely been to a place so wild, and I had never been to a place that all at once was this beautiful, this spectacular, and this unheard-of. Such a place ought to be a national park, be celebrated in adventure travel catalogues, be the subject of glowing reports in magazines. Yet all I could think of were my problems: my pregnant wife, far away; my face, swollen and throbbing; and my skin, which I was trying desperately to shield from the sun.

We scrambled back down from the crumbling rock and retraced our steps over the iron flow. The implausibility of having found that single tern's egg was reinforced by the fact that we didn't see it again, despite descending in exactly the same way. When we arrived back at the raft, it was limp, even though we'd been gone only a few hours. I wondered if it were going to just fall apart on the river—crumble, sink.

We flopped in the raft, untied it, and let it drift. We were so hot that we drank as much glacial water from the lake as our stomachs could handle, which wasn't all that much, because glacial water doesn't really taste very good, mixed too much with particles of glacier, which you can feel on your teeth, on your tongue, and in your throat. The cooling currents of the water made for a perfect climate, but the raft kept drifting into the center of the lake because of the northerly wind. Sadly, we had to sit up and paddle quietly home.

I knew in the morning we were going to retreat to the other end of the lake. That would be the first step on the journey back to Maine, to my wife, my family, and my new baby. The thought of heading home cheered me up, as though I were almost there. I got out a picture of Pat I kept in my wallet and smiled foolishly at it.

———

In the tent I figured the distances we had to travel, starting that morning. Where we were going was still unclear, to be determined by whether or not the sea kayak appeared. We wouldn't know until we got down to the Stikine, and then we would have a choice—maybe—of continuing down the Stikine or finding a way to descend the Sheslay, the Inklin, the Taku, then Taku Inlet. From Chutine Lake to Wrangell was 180 miles by river; the other route would be nearly 225.

Now, for the first time, it occurred to me to wonder whether the Chutine was really runnable. I had been assuming, without thinking about the assumption, that it was. Flying up the Chutine three days before, it had looked okay—there were no obvious waterfalls, no obstructions that would block the entire river, but I had been wrong about this sort of thing before.

In August of 1982 I loitered in Anchorage for an extra week after guiding on the Kobuk. I always hated to leave Anchorage, not because it is such a great town, but because it is the gateway to the rest of Alaska. The old joke is, What's the best thing about Anchorage? The answer: From there it's only a short drive to Alaska.

After five years of running the Kobuk, I was looking for another river to try. Any river is good, but a new river is best. I went downtown to the Anchorage Public Library and reviewed maps. The river needed to have several things: to be long enough for a commercial trip—at least a hundred miles; to be well out into the bush but not so high up in mountains that it would be a torrent rather than a river; and to be accessible, which meant it had to have good gravel nearby, or a lake.

One river had the right features: the Skwentna. It started at the base of glaciers in the Alaska Range and traveled alongside twelve-thousand-foot peaks before turning to the east toward the broader terrain of the Cook Inlet area. I could see from maps that the headwaters were in a wide valley, so there was the possibility of gravel bars for shuttles. From the headwaters of the Skwentna down to the confluence with the Yentna River, where there was a village and a landing strip, was about a hundred miles, long enough to make a decent trip. On paper it looked perfect, but I had to see it, and so I and another guide, Lisa Moorhead, bribed a pilot friend of Lisa's with airplane fuel to take us to look in his Cub.

We flew west across Cook Inlet and up the Chakachatna River, then swung around the foot of the Spurr glacier falling off the sides of volcanic Mt. Spurr, where we could see puffs of smoke erupting occasionally, and headed north into the valley of the Skwentna.

Everything about the river and canyon was perfect. On one side, the east, mountains seemed to shoot straight up, leaving a white vapor trail of snow and ice behind. The lower slopes of the mountains gently curved to end in the valley below us, which was broad and green. There was plenty of gravel, although it was hard to tell if there was enough to land on. The river began somewhere—its source was hard to spot—and after a dozen miles or so, the various threads of it joined together to make a single rope that led out of the broad valley.

A dense forest crept to the edge of the river; the canyon tightened—and my pulse sped up, as a tight canyon always means whitewater, obstructions, dangers. We flew directly above the river, following it downstream. I could see whitewater below me, looking like riffles. The river seemed swift but easy. I wished I could have started right then, but I had to wait another year to come back with a small group of people who had paid for the privilege of making the first rafting descent of the Skwentna River.

The Skwentna turned out to be just what we'd hoped. The only problem was the difficulty of reading whitewater from a moving plane, even a relatively slow one such as the one we had borrowed. What from the air looked like riffles, turned out to be rapids, and for some reason it had never occurred to me to review the topographic maps I owned, which obviously showed that the river, once it left the broad valley, dropped at a rate of nearly a hundred feet per mile, which in river terms is a screamer. The Colorado in Grand Canyon averages only about eight feet per mile; the Stanislaus, twenty-five feet; and the Tuolumne River, thirty-five feet per mile.

As a result, the Skwentna's upper stretch was fast and steady, and there were millions of rocks to avoid. We had to stop several times to scout, and at one scout, as the other guide, John Storrer, and I were tramping through the bear-infested blueberry bushes that edged each side of the river, I let out a sigh as we faced yet another tricky pitch of water.

"It sure didn't look like this from the air," I said, announcing the obvious.

John gave me a look that suggested he'd put himself in the hands of an idiot. "Didn't you look at a map?" he asked.

I grinned. "Nope," I replied.

John shook his head, which was covered by a big, brown cowboy hat that had a hole where a black bear had bit it the day before—fortunately, when his head was elsewhere. "'No rapids,' you said. 'Nothing but riffles.'" He was repeating what I'd told him over the winter, when I suggested he join me on the trip.

"Well, okay, a slight mistake," I admitted. "Adds to the fun, though, right?" I didn't need to encourage him; he was as thrilled by the river as I was. Still, the experience taught me a lesson about thinking one could read rivers from the air.

The mosquitoes were so bad that last morning on Chutine Beach that I had to wear two shirts to keep them away, sit in the smoke coming off our morning fire in the oppressive sun, and feel cut off entirely from the experience of lake and shore. We packed up quickly, and after one more stroll in the ridiculously grand setting, we tossed our packs into the raft and shoved off.

The mosquitoes vanished as soon as we hit the lake. We paddled lazily for a bit, aiming for the western shore of the lake, but the wind from the drainage of Chutine Creek was blowing us south faster than we could paddle west. Max got out a rain fly with cords attached at every corner, and we rigged a sort of sail. We tied the fly to the handles of our paddles and jammed the blades between the thwarts and the side tubes, making the *Dunny* look like a dhow. The cords gave us the equivalent of halyards, by which we could bring in or let out the makeshift sail. Placing our backs to the wind, we leaned against the upwind tube, braced ourselves, and let out on the fly; gradually the wind filled it. The sensation was that of sailing, more or less. We pulled in on the sail at the bottom, adjusted the angle of the paddle, tried lifting or dropping one paddle relative to the other, and scooted down the lake like a big, bulky, gray, rubber yacht. The only thing we couldn't control very well was the exact direction we were going. We had to go with the wind, which in this case was northeast to southwest, shoving us a few hundred yards to the west of where we wanted to go.

This fly-as-spinnaker arrangement invited a return to our debate on the topic of control. The situation reinforced both of our positions: mine, that we were in control of our sailing, with our control limited only by our skills and equipment and enough to achieve our objective—that is, returning to our base camp on the blond beach; Max's, that while we might think we were controlling the situation, the control was only partial and temporary, and any control that is partial and temporary can't be real, can't be called control.

"Well, if we're not in control," I said, lowering the paddle so that one end of the sail dropped, luffing in the breeze, "then this won't make any difference, will it?" The raft slogged to a halt and bobbed on the waves.

Max laughed. "Pick that up, dang it, or we'll fry out here." I lifted the paddle and the wind grabbed hold of us again and we surged ahead.

"It's just that kind of attitude that screws everything up," he asserted. "We think we're in control of everything, the world, each other, and so we meddle around in things and mess them all up, then say that if only we had better techniques or knew more we would have been able to do better, and so we ought to meddle more, rather than take our stupid hands off of it all."

"So what are we supposed to do?" I asked. "Give up? Should we try to solve problems, or just leave them? All of those people struggling to get by, or with jobs that kill them, should we throw our hands up and tell them, 'Sorry, we're not in control?'"

"It'd be nice to think we could do something, but don't you see? Thinking we can do something, and that we have to, has made us muck around in the past, and nothing gets better."

"Don't we have a responsibility to try and correct it?" I asked with growing frustration.

"No, we don't," said Max, laughing again. The more impassioned I became, the more Max laughed. Ordinarily this might have been cause for murder. "It's too bad things are screwed up, but they're screwed up because we think we have to control them, and because we try to, and that's why they're screwed up. So we ought to leave it all alone."

"That's great in the abstract," I said as the *Dunny* plowed through a wave, "but what are you going to do when some guy rips off your mountain bike? Nothing? Not try to 'control' that situation? Besides," I went on, getting wound up now, "I take the tragic view—even if we're going to fail, we have to try."

"You're right," Max said. "It is tragic; the whole thing's tragic," he concluded, and he adjusted the paddle so it stood upright again.

"Aha!" I crowed; "There you go again, trying to control the wind," but Max just chuckled, so I gave up.

The wind, over which we did or did not have much control, had forced us into the western shore a quarter mile north of where we wanted to be. We had to abandon the sail, which was painful, since we had been comfortable lying there against the tubes, adjusting the sail from time to time, feeling the wind on our necks. It's too bad one can't sail a raft down a wilderness lake all day, every day.

We came to the blond beach and parked the *Oyster Dunny* and began the process of loading for the river, which waited for us only a mile or so to the south. We had talked of spending one more night at the lake, but that was earlier, and now the understanding seemed to be that we would head out. It was high noon, and there was plenty of time to eat lunch, rig for the river, and still enter the swift water that day. An exciting thought: moving water.

We hummed around the camp, eating lunch and rearranging our gear. I had brought a section of an old cargo net, a piece of thick nylon webbing, like the ones in old World War II movies that the soldiers use to scramble down from a ship. I tied the cargo net across the back of the raft; then put on it the metal box containing perishable food, along with the pump, the repair kit, and some of our river bags and food bags; and covered the pile with a tarp, over which I ran lines.

We tied the half-Nautiraid across the front thwart and used carabiners to clip the river bags to the D-rings. We would sit in the center area, between the thwarts, one of us on each side, and this area we kept clear. The shotgun went on top of the gear pile in the rear.

It was a delicate moment. Now that I was leaving, I felt the pull of the place where I stood—of the glacier up the valley from the beach; of Mt. Chutine towering over us; of the headwaters of the Barrington, still calling to me, untouched; of the lake, the strangest-looking body of water I had ever seen.

But staying wasn't an option, so we pushed off and headed our tiny, lonely craft toward the small hole in the trees through which we would escape.

5 *Down River*

... a dream of childhood and one as powerful as the erotic dreams of
adolescence—floating down the river.
— Edward Abbey, *Desert Solitaire*

Boundary Creek on the Middle Fork. Lee's Ferry on the Colorado; for
the Tuolumne, Meral's Pool; Camp Nine on the Stanislaus; the Rogue's
Almeda Bar. Walker Lake on the Kobuk, Harris Station for the Kennebec,
the bridge at Rome for the Owyhee, Corn Creek on the Main Salmon.
Gravel bars along the Noatak or Skwentna or Tatshenshinni or Alsek.

These are put-ins, places where one begins the journey down the river.
Every runnable river has one, of course, yet they are not common: they are
confluences, estuaries, the interstices between river life and non-river life.

Utterly different, river and shore, as different—and conjoined—as the
other great antitheses: sea and land, heaven and hell, earth and sky, inno-
cence and experience. The adventure narratives of the eighteenth and nine-
teenth centuries took place on the sea, from Defoe to Melville to Dana to
Conrad to Stevenson; except for *Huckleberry Finn* and *Heart of Darkness*,
the river hasn't been a setting for equivalent adventures. This isn't the fault
of the rivers, but of writers who haven't figured out what messages rivers
bring, what metaphors and symbols they provide.

The river is a vein, a cord, a canal, a colon, a clock. Annie Dillard says,
"The creeks are the world with all its stimulus and beauty." It is a simple
miracle, the nature of rivers: water gathers high, searches for the lowest
spot in the landscape, and, having found it, exploits it, then flows and flows.

Rivers simply move from high to low and therefore are on a journey that is both finite and circular. A river comes to an end, but Rivers participate in the infinite as rain and snow, then moving water again. Once, I scattered the ashes of a friend into the Rogue River, at the upstream end of a place called Solitude Bar—a prayer to the infinite as expressed by rivers.

The ocean is too much, too vast, too brutal. It is our experience of space, the medium that lets us know what space is like. Rivers are an experience of time. The river is more human than the ocean, limited like humans are, yet sweeping forward in its implacable way, like time itself sweeping past. We are proportioned to rivers: they correspond to our bodies in ways the ocean doesn't. To be on a river is to enter a new but familiar rhythm. That rhythm remains in you even when you're away from rivers, just as the felt rhythm of a poem lingers in you even when the words are lost. This is the pull of moving water. The pull is a palpable thing, a physical sensation: a longing, a sensation of flow.

Put-ins come in various forms. Some are paved ramps, some are trails ending in a tiny beach, and some, as on the Chutine, are exit streams. Even exit streams are varied: some are brush-choked threads out of a lake, and others are wide, smooth pathways; some drop off precipitously, a falls, and others slowly wind their way downward, outward. But all exit streams have at least one thing in common: movement. At the lip of the exit, the current begins, tugging on you, no matter how slowly. It is one of those dividing lines in life, between two radically different things—flat water and moving water.

The transition causes vertigo. You feel yourself being drawn down, and unlike the vertigo of high places, here it is okay to leap. As Max and I approached that dividing line on the Chutine, I felt the usual mix of thrill and trepidation. I tried to block out any unhappy thoughts, thoughts such as, "Maybe this won't work" or "Maybe we'll have to hike out" or "Maybe the river disappears ahead." I felt the pull of the creek. We were locked in now—if we were going to leave this place, we would have to float out.

The Chutine was barely wide enough for the *Dunny*, and the first hundred yards were straight and fast. Then we came to a turn. "Back-paddle," I said, and Max bent backwards with his paddle. I did the same, trying to slow the raft so we could see what would unfold as we came around the corner.

The first corner was clear, but another corner followed right beyond it, and the river swept us past them, not quite out of control but on the edge, so there wasn't time to look around or to plan but only to react as the river took us around one turn, and the next, then the next.

For forty-five minutes we raced along too fast for anything but paddling, trying to see around blind turns, trying to predict what was ahead. It wasn't whitewater but swift water, and completely engaging. I felt my confidence seeping back, being restored by contact with moving water. This was familiar: the sensation of being drawn downriver, the look of the water off the sides of the raft, the feel of the raft responding to choppy little waves.

I angled the *Oyster Dunny* into a tiny break in the grasses along the shore and grabbed a branch. I was puffing, and Max had a string of sweat dripping down his cheek. "Yes!" I cheered. Max laughed and nodded and wiped his face.

For the first time I was able to look around. Right above us were peaks with snow trapped on the higher ridges. There were wildflowers and grasses along the river, fed by both the river and the streams falling through the ravines on either side; the landscape was green and fresh, colored by water.

"This is an amazing place," Max offered. I agreed. We got out the maps and tried to figure out how far we had come and where we were along the stream. By triangulating with peaks and taking positional compass readings, I was able to tell that we had no idea where we were. We had been moving fast, but on a river that twisted and turned radically, we could have come five miles or two. It didn't matter, of course; we weren't going anywhere, just downstream.

We pushed out into the stream again. The first flush from the lake had slowed. The river braided now as the canyon eased back. Braiding forces one into the act of making choices. This is true whether you are going upstream, like Sid in his riverboats, or downstream, like us. The sight of a river that has divided itself into half a dozen separate channels, each of which is blind—that is, you can't see the end of it—can be intimidating.

When you approach a braided section, your eye scans the area, and you might see how the water humps up in the middle channel and falls off to either side, which means that the water in the center is liable to be shallow and the water to the sides will be swifter and deeper, but at the same time, you can see that the center channels are clear, whereas the ones to the side may or may not be. So sometimes you go with your instincts and take a chance.

Our river was still shifting and turning like mad, dividing into braids, each of which was skinny and had water rushing through it very fast. About a half hour after our first stop, we came around a corner to face a choice of four channels. The ones off to the left were clearly no good, being too small and too choked with the sweepers that fall down in spring, when the ice shears away the banks of the rivers. The channel in the center was clear, but the water was thin, and I decided we would probably ground out there. The only other choice was the far right branch; it had the most water moving into it but was a blind turn, the choice that one most avoids in channel choosing.

I wasn't worried; so far every channel had been fine, every choice the right one. Each successful turn of the river, each wise choice of a channel, confirmed my abilities as a river man. I picked the right-hand channel boldly.

Naturally it was blocked, by a sweeper that had fallen from the main shore all the way onto the island that formed the braid.

"Back-paddle!" I yelled. "Back! back! back!"

"Oh boy," Max chimed in, leaning back on his paddle, laying himself nearly horizontal on the raft to do so.

I had visions of perching on the tree, half of the boat over the limb and the other half under, with Max and I trapped in the boat under the log or floating—boatless—away. An ugly vision.

The raft crept slowly toward the log, a magnet drawing us. We edged sideways across the braid and managed to land at a break in the constant vegetation on shore. We grabbed hold of some willows, then leapt off the boat and clung to it from shore.

My confidence oozed away. Every move becomes magnified when you are on a river, every facet of your personality and your life becomes drawn in vivid colors—you become vividly what you are. And if you make a wrong choice, you become a Person Who Makes Wrong Choices.

We were going to have to portage the *Dunny*. We untied all of the gear, which we had tied in only a couple of hours earlier, and packed it along a muddy path we created through the willows to a spot about fifty feet away where we could put the raft back into the creek. About halfway down the path, the mud became a swamp, which we sank into as we carried river bags, boxes, and paddles. After all of the gear was stationed at the new location, we looked at the raft. The *Oyster Dunny* was empty now, naked except for the net and a few lines left strung on her. We could either carry her though this narrow, swampy, awkward path or do the safe thing and deflate her, roll her up, and spend an extra hour moving her that way. We lifted the *Dunny* onto our heads and dragged her down the path, the sharp ends of willow stubs jabbing the raft as we dragged.

After checking downstream for more braids, we pushed off again, a little more subdued than before but glad to be on the smooth of the river instead of the messy path. We zigged and zagged our way down several more miles of fast water, the river turning rhythmically, the swirling mountains lost to us because we couldn't pay attention to them, and then we began looking for a camp.

I could see on the map that a drainage, Dirst Creek, came in from the south about thirteen miles downstream from the lake. It would be a day's float from there to the foot of Mt. Barrington. In late afternoon we passed Dirst Creek on our right and could look up the canyon from which it exited. It was a long, narrow defile, a mix of dark tones and rock and ice. The lower skirts of the canyon spread out in a gentle fan, and above them were the vertical spires of the mountains that held an attractive glacier that formed the creek. One could break down such a view into its parts and ex-plain its appeal—the combination of vertical (mountains) with horizontal (the floodplain), of rock with ice, solids with liquids, dark with light—and all of that would be true, but the eighteenth-century nature appreciators had it right when they referred to such views as "sublime."

We pulled into a long, smooth gravel bar on the left. There were a couple of tall cottonwood trees lying flat on the bar, their bark stripped off from the force of the river and ice passing over them. It had the look of a good camp: the cottonwoods would give us shelter from the river winds; the gravel at the water's edge was smooth and easy to walk on, and we could lift a very saggy *Oyster Dunny* onto it; there were little islands of sand among the gravel and cottonwoods, which would make a cooking spot and a place for the tent; there was even plenty of driftwood around, wedged into the cottonwoods—perfect. Across the way was a row of cottonwoods, alders, and some pines in various stages of tilting into the river. Their roots below the level of the bank were exposed, and we wondered how they could stay upright with so little purchase on the soil. Indeed, while we sat at our fire after dinner, we heard a crack, a whoosh, and then a whap, like a thunderous beaver's tail slapping the water.

A nice downstream breeze kept the bar clear of insects, too. The usual rule is that the winds in a river canyon blow upstream, from late morning until the sun sets. In the north the winds are more variable. We had been leading a downriver wind all day, and I couldn't understand it until we were here, looking back up the canyon of Dirst Creek. The winds were coming from its glacier, a breeze cooling on the surface of the ice, then sweeping down it, down the creek and into the Chutine. Max predicted that when the sun went down, the winds would drop, and they did.

———

The Yukon was a skein of ice from late October until May, and Dawson was almost completely cut off from the rest of the world. When the ice finally went out, the town was naturally anxious for supplies, which were then worth more than the gold in the ground. The first boat to arrive after ice-out was feted, and to be the pilot of such a boat was a feather in your cap, a notch on your gun, a sign of your stature as a river man.

On June 8 of 1898, the *May West* steamed into Dawson ahead of everyone else. Its only cargo was sixteen barrels of whiskey, which sold for a dollar a glass like lightning. No one seemed to mind that the *May West* wasn't carrying food or equipment or medical supplies. The arrival of whiskey was a civic celebration, heralding the end of winter and the arrival—soon, the Dawsonites hoped—of more substantial goods.

Sid owned the *May West*, and the story goes that he was captain when she arrived in 1898. This image, of Sid showing up with a boatload of whiskey, is perfect: full of joie de vivre, a roustabout's sensibility, a lusty and manly disregard for the practical in favor of carpe diem. Too bad, then, that the story isn't true. Sid didn't buy the *May West* until 1899, from the Royal Canadian Mounted Police, who had taken it over because of some failing (selling whiskey?) on the part of the previous owners.

After returning to Seattle in late fall of 1898 from his debacle in Nome, Sid heard that a large steamer, the *James Domville*, was available to be chartered in the Yukon Territory but that other parties were interested also.

Since it was winter, and the *Domville* was locked in ice at Whitehorse Rapids, and the owners were in Dawson, Sid needed to get to Dawson before anyone else. He came back up to Skagway in midwinter, bought a dog team and sled, and went over the pass and down the ice on the Yukon, a thousand miles of it, to Dawson, where he agreed to pay $11,000 for the contract on the *James Domville*.

This same adventure appears in another version, set a year later, when Sid and Hill were supposed to have made their way to Dawson on bicycles (on bicycles?), riding 470 miles in winter, on ice (on ice?), to secure the lease of a different steamer, the *Florence S.* When they got to Dawson, they made that same $11,000 bid on the *Florence S.* and, having been accepted, set out to find a way to raise the money, which they did not have.

Their solution was original: they created an imaginary gold strike, selling tickets to that location after spreading the rumor. The site of this phony strike was the Koyukuk River, another tributary of the Yukon, hundreds of miles downstream from Dawson.

Having sold enough tickets to pay their obligation to the owners of the *Florence S.*, they set off for the Koyukuk, hoping that somehow a miracle would save them. As they approached the mouth of the Koyukuk, they hailed an Indian paddling alongshore in a canoe and asked him where the river was. The Indian pointed at a drainage coming in just downstream and supposedly said, "There him is." The moment had come; they were about to be exposed. Just then the Indian turned back to the men in the boat and asked whether they were going upstream to join the new gold strike.

Sid promptly sank the *James Domville* in the spring of 1899 on the Thirty Mile River. He also wrecked the *Florence S.* on the same river on July 20, 1900, then dropped the *May West* (renamed the *Vidette*) on a far-upstream tributary (the Pelly River), raised her only to sink her again on Lake Laberge, and finished off this string of bad work by crashing the *La France* on the Thirty Mile, which clearly is a river he should have avoided. This would all be comical if it weren't for the fate of the *Florence S.*, for in that sinking, three people died.

Riverboats perched and sank with alarming frequency along the Yukon and its tributaries in those days, but this accident must have been special, because an inquiry was launched. The account of the trial was published in a Seattle paper. In that story, Yorke Barrington said, "I have all along known . . . that Sid could not have been to blame in the matter. He is much too careful a man for that. As it turns out, he was not at the wheel at all when the accident occurred. . . . My brother, who was owner and pilot of the steamer, had been continuously on duty for twenty-four hours, and had turned the wheel over to the captain just before the steamer capsized."

An Inspector Starnes, who was in charge of the investigation, objected that "while there was plenty of evidence to show carelessness and neglect of duty on the part of someone he could find nothing to sustain the charges against Barrington." Though not exactly a ringing endorsement, this was enough to get Sid back on the water.

In 1900 Sid had his greatest triumph, although this one, too, is mired in murkiness. A steamer, the *Clifford Sifton*, had been working the flat waters above Whitehorse, in Marsh Lake. In the midst of the 1900 season, the boat was sold, and the new owner intended to take her below Whitehorse to work the more profitable route between Dawson and Lake Laberge. There was some talk of dismantling the boat, but she was large, a double-stacker, so the decision was made to run her instead through the whitewater of Miles Canyon, Five Fingers Rapid, and Whitehorse Rapids.

Since this was by far the largest steamer to attempt the canyon and only the second or sixth sternwheeler (or fourth, depending upon who is telling the story: as one historian points out, "many a steamboat captain claimed to be the first to bring his boat through the series of rapids") to have made a try, it was a noteworthy event.

In her hagiography, Willoughby quotes a mate who tells the tale. When Sid agreed to take the *Clifford Sifton* through, "the eyes of the whole country were on him!" claims the mate.

"Just before he was ready to start through he pulled a stunt that set the whole river talking. He fastened baled hay all around that steamer! Then, with only four of us aboard to help him, he threw her wide open and swung her into that roaring, watery hole! . . . That was the greatest feat of piloting ever performed on the Yukon."

Hill Barrington, at ninety-five, still remembered the run. He told a newspaper reporter, "With a defiant blast on the whistle, [we] started downstream, the big sternwheel thrashing in reverse. The available population of Whitehorse lined the cliff edge to see the smash.

"'We never once touched the walls,' Hill said.

"[We] swooped down the canyon in reverse, swinging the boat around at the bends and steaming full speed to avoid the eddies and turmoil, then in reverse again. A fraction of a second delay or hesitation would have been fatal.

"'One ship, one mile, three men, three minutes and three thousand dollars,' Hill says."

In 1900 Sid and brothers Hill and Harry formed the Yukon Sidestream Navigation Company. For the next fourteen years, as steamboats gave way to diesel- and gas-powered boats, Sid and his brothers bulled their way up the major tributaries of the upper Yukon: the Stewart, the Pelly, the White, the Porcupine.

The accidents and adventures became less frequent after the turn of the century, although at one point during his time on the Yukon, Sid saved 128 passengers from freezing on the last trip out from Dawson, for which the passengers gave him a gold medallion with an image of a riverboat, a diamond for its searchlight, a ruby for the port light, and an emerald for the starboard. About 1901 Sid met his future wife, Hazel Delisle, at a landing along the Yukon River. "He chanced to set eyes on her as she came aboard his boat at some river landing in Alaska and his fate was sealed then and there," wrote Scoop Grealey, a Puget Sound newspaperman. "'That's the girl for me,' he said—and later on that same day he asked her to marry him. From then on till the end of their days together they were inseparable," which, while not physically accurate, was emotionally true. In 1903 they had their only child, a son named York.

About 1909 Sid went into partnership with Charles Binkley, a shipbuilder, to form the Binkley & Barrington (B&B) Transportation Company. They built their first boat in 1909—the first of what would become a fleet, all named *Hazel B.* after Hazel Barrington. They were distinguished from one another only by being numbered 1, 2, or 3, but even this didn't solve the confusion, for there were two 2s and two 3s.

By 1914 gold production had declined in the Yukon. After the excitement of Miles Canyon, of swapping gold claims for steamers, of losing them gambling, of sinking them on new rivers, and earning the admiration of the Territory, Sid gave up on the Yukon. He knew the river too well by then, and perhaps it was too far away from winter quarters in Puget Sound. York would have been twelve, and that might have had something to do with the decision as well. Sid and Binkley spent the 1914 and 1915 seasons northwest of Anchorage, on the Susitna River, where they carried freight to support the construction of the Alaska Railroad. After that, Sid went looking for a new home. Perhaps he, too, pored over maps or listened to the stories of other river men, but somehow he found what he was looking for, and he appeared on the Alaska panhandle in 1916. As the mate in "Champion Swift-Water Pilot of the North" says, "What he likes best is a new river."

After the gear was up on our beach on the Chutine, I made a fire pit, then gathered firewood from the piles of driftwood that littered the beach. One of the pleasures of guiding is the odd way in which memories are generated: by a breeze, a rock, a particular configuration of mountain and shadow. Every time I gather firewood along a river, for instance, I think of Matt Murphy, a legendary guide I knew when I was starting. Matt had guided since the late '60s (the dawn of rafting). He had a long, handlebar moustache and a braying sort of laugh that he used as a weapon. It was the sort of laugh that diminished people, put them on the defensive. It made argument impossible, because when he'd score a point he'd follow it up with a laugh, which was meant to signal that he had won. Arguing with him was hard anyhow, since he was a clever fellow.

Matt was the first guide I knew who was a victim of the two dangers of the profession: burned out by guiding and ruined by the seduction of it. A guide's life is a good one, but intense. The intensity comes from the rivers, of course—the adrenaline rush of the rapids, the experience of living on river time—and from the pressures of dealing with people; you are continually meeting new groups, making new connections, learning again how to relate to this particular set. There are few circumstances more intimate than that of guiding a river trip: once you head down the river, who else do people have but the guides and each other? Great friendships are made, and bitter enmities, and romances unfold—just like real life, only more concentrated. After a while, the intensity of life as a guide wears the guides down, especially in the West, where the rivers and trips are longer, from a weekend to a week to nearly three weeks in the Grand Canyon. The repetition of tasks also wears guides down; they seem to go on and on, numbing in their mindlessness. By the end of the season, the thought of one more trip can be crushing.

All guides eventually burn out, hot wire in one way or another. I have seen guides flailing at each other, seen them so sullen they could barely speak, getting drunk and ugly. Back in Fairbanks after my first trip on the Kobuk with Bo Mandeville, sitting in the dirt outside a friend's house on the outskirts of town, late at night: we leaned against our gear in the perpetual twilight, drinking most of a bottle of Jim Beam. We drank and talked, and Bo became more and more agitated, until he was accusing me of several failings of spirit, none of which I remember but all of which were probably true, and he took an ammo box—the small, metal, army-surplus boxes that are guide-equivalents of purses, in which guides carry things that need to be protected from water (mostly condoms and dope)—and swung it at me. I laughed at the first swing, thinking he was kidding, that this was one of those wacky drunken jokes, but the second swing was closer, and I began to get to my feet, and he did too. His third swing was wild and pulled him off his feet and onto his back, where he stayed, laughing.

The other problem, being ruined by guiding, is more existential. For many guides, guiding is the equivalent of working at a summer camp: an interlude, an interesting and entertaining pause between college and graduate school. But there were others for whom guiding was a life. For them it was part of a mix that might include ski patrolling, or extended aimless travels, or collecting unemployment, or working as an EMT, or guiding somewhere else in the off season—in Costa Rica or New Zealand or Chile.

When I became a guide, I realized I had found something I had been looking for without knowing I was looking for it. My own weird little niche, peopled by other dropouts, who seemed interesting, at least to me. Several had been college athletes; others were the wiry, hairy sort that the times bred, with ropy muscles, no fat, long stringy hair. For both men and women there were earrings and ponytails and tattoos and unself-conscious nudity. They were a new sort, I thought: not the Haight-Ashbury sort of dropout, more like athletes who had decided to compete in a different sport. They weren't devoted to drugs and sex and rock and roll, but drugs and sex and rock and roll were the background music to the main story, the rivers. What guiding gave them was the freedom of the rivers and woods, an unusual way to live for a while, a lack of complex obligations.

My guiding life, then, started with a combination that aided my ruination. One was my age, nineteen, when to discover something completely different from any previous experience gave it the glow that any dramatic new thing—love, sex, a skill, a knowledge, an experience—has hovering around it; another was the nature of the occupation, with its modest danger, spectacular setting, and the simple joy of moving water. To commute to my job, I cruised through the springtime foothills, and while I was at work, all that was required of me was to start at one elevation in a canyon and go downhill to another spot.

Finding this life made me feel as though I had entered a parallel, better universe, and so, like many guides, for a time I was ruined for other work. Unless you are devoted enough to those things that can be had from conventional occupations—money, security, a future, a family (or at least a relationship)—guiding corrupts you, because all of those are in jeopardy when you are a guide. I guided fitfully throughout the '80s, my second decade of guiding, doing at least one or two long trips every year, occasionally working on a river for a month or so, because I couldn't find anything else that gave me the same combination that guiding did. Guiding is part performance, part sport, part bacchanal, part Thoreau, part Twain—and nothing is much like it.

Everything else seemed pale. Although perhaps not everything, for I had exalted moments while snow camping, or sea kayaking, or even teaching, but they weren't the same. I avoided getting married, delayed professional life (yet later treasured being married and found the professorial life satisfying), saved time every summer to guide a little. Gradually I had to put guiding aside, and when I did, it was only with much twisting and shrugging and itching, as though normal life were a hair shirt. I sacrificed guiding to have a stable life, but I still felt the lure of moving water.

The perfect piece of firewood that I was looking for along the Chutine, and which made me think of Matt Murphy and burned-out legendary boatmen, would be, in Matt's words, "as big around as your forearm and about two feet long." This type of firewood was embarrassingly plentiful along the banks of the Chutine. As I picked up the wood, I felt the thousands of other pieces I had handled in my guiding life.

At last I was at home. Home, a sensation I'd been waiting for: a broad sandy beach, a river flowing past, the views of a river camp—grand views up- and downriver. I swiveled my head back and forth, trying to take it all in. Still not possible, even though I felt as though all of it were pouring into me.

Max started talking after dinner, confirming what I already knew. He was upset. Something had been bothering him, but I didn't know what. By then I had become convinced of our incompatibility. Max had some of the same qualities as Bo Mandeville: he was in a difficult place in his life, with a tendency toward emotional peaks and valleys and needing to stay on those peaks, for fear of sliding into the valleys. I had somehow brought Max sliding down, and he wanted to talk about it.

We were sitting on ammo boxes by the fire, keeping a low profile because the wind off the glacier hadn't stopped yet. Max began by saying, "You know, you really piss me off," and it was obviously true, since he was squirming angrily on the ammo box—my ammo box, I might add—and clasping his hands in a way that communicated anger.

"Oh, yes?" I replied, stirring the coals in the fire with a stick, trying to sound unconcerned. This was all too familiar, someone wanting to discuss his anger at me, with me. I'd rather he talk to someone else about it, but no one ever does.

"Yeah," Max said, squirming. "You think you have answers to things, and you think I don't, and that pisses me off."

Here was a puzzle. Should I confess that I thought there were some things I knew, or should I protest that, really, I knew nothing?

"Well, what do you want me to say, Max?" I asked, throwing my stick into the fire. "Do you want me to believe what you believe, that we don't control anything, that we're all helpless? That's not what I think. I'm not going to say that just to please you."

Max seemed taken aback at first, but with a sinking feeling I knew I was trapped. A little smile appeared on his face, and he pushed me lightly on the shoulder. "No, that's not what I want," he said. "I want you to show some emotion, some anger. I'm tired of you being so level about everything. See, you were mad; I wanted you to get mad, lose a little control."

"Oh fuck me," I said, sick of this. When I'd been considering this trip, it hadn't occurred to me that my partner would be the sort for whom conversations of this sort would be important. And for the next two weeks and several hundred miles we were stuck with each other.

During the rest of the evening, we accused each other of certain flaws, including being shallowly intellectual (me), or self-absorbed (him). Max talked about his family and how his father had died, and about his work as an academic, and about his frustrations with his life, his kids, and his first wife, and about the changes he was going through. I confessed my doubts about the wisdom of this trip. Eventually we got quiet.

That night I saw a bald eagle fly close by. It was flying downriver, against the wind, and at times it lowered its legs into the stiff breeze, almost as if it were preparing to land, yet it was fifty or a hundred feet up in the air. I couldn't decide exactly what this gesture was about: some technique for maintaining balance in the face of a wind, I suppose. Interpreting the gestures of others is a tricky business but impossible to resist.

It was an ideal morning to sit in the sand, staring across at the tilting cottonwoods. Clear, cool, no breeze, no mosquitoes. I worried a little about what we would do when we got downstream to the Stikine. Hackett and Sheslay, or Stikine and Wrangell Sound? I didn't want to care too much: everything here looked too good for such worries. The bar was littered with fireweed, the light was as crisp as a new sheet of paper, the river flowing past sounded like my blood, as though my veins were outside my body. I wrote in my journal "cottonwoods low, the evergreens, the valley filled with snow and ice, the rock, the colours, the gendarmes, peaks and pinnacles— hard country, the hardest I've ever seen, in all of the ways country can be hard" and it wasn't a complaint.

Max told a story about spirit dances, in which the native dancers assume the posture of an animal—a bear, for instance—and hold it until they feel the spirit of the bear enter them. I told my own spirit story.

"One night I was camped along the Stanislaus and woke up in the middle of the night because I was thirsty. I was going to get some water from the river.

"The moon had just gone behind the limestone cliff across from camp, so the river was in shadow, but the shore where I slept was in moonlight.

"I heard laughter, and when I looked out in the river, I saw two people talking and splashing in the water. This was the middle of the night, remember, and the river is cold, even in summer. I blinked and looked again, but it still was two naked people walking in the river, right out at the edge where a submerged gravel bar ended and dropped off into deep water. They weren't any of the people on the trip. I remember how happy they sounded. The moonlight was in my eyes, and the river makes a laughing sound there anyhow, so I thought I was making it all up, but no matter how much I slapped myself awake or shook myself, I couldn't make the two people go away.

"I wasn't going to get any water from a river that had ghosts in it, so I just went back to sleep. In the morning I asked around, but no one had been up."

On the water we had no leisure, as we needed to be paddling most of the time, to keep from careening into shore. The river had lost some of its anxious energy, but it was still swift. The turns were more gradual—there were actual eddies at times—and we could look about, although I was often absorbed in the task of keeping Max going. Max would become distracted by his surroundings and forget about the river, and I had to remind him that the river needed us. I reflected, aloud, on the fact that this would be a very difficult descent without whitewater skills. "Max, you'd be toast without me on this river." He chuckled but otherwise didn't acknowledge that I was saving him.

We saw some salmon making their way upstream. They wriggled in the shallows, their spines breaking the surface. I don't understand why I have the reactions I do to the animals of the kingdom. Salmon, for example: the sight of their wiggling tails pleases me, makes me want to giggle. It is such an unhuman gesture, like nothing we are capable of, except perhaps for the rippling gesture of a dancer's arms in a certain kind of dance. A powerful gesture, and somehow soothing. Caribou, too—the only animal I've ever wanted to hunt, even though they are royal animals, a pure pleasure to look upon. One year I came across herds of caribou along the Noatak River, hundreds swimming the river or bunched on gravel bars. The males were in velvet, the blood from their new racks pouring down their heads. The caribou were a wonderful and unfamiliar sight. I can't explain this desire, then, to shoot one.

We paddled down the Chutine for two hours that morning. The wind, another downstream breeze, came up. We turned a confusing corner, where there were so many things to look at that my eye and brain were over-whelmed. There were the mountains downstream, marching on and on, each one different, and the left side of the river, the north, was dry and rocky, while the right was more alpine, with snow and glaciers; along both sides of the river were wild scrambles of trees and logs, some on shore and some in the water, some on islands, and some making islands. It was im-possible to tell what was a channel and what was a creek.

At one of those channels there was movement—a little black bear cub, rummaging about some logs up a back channel from the main river. As we drew closer he got bigger, until he became an adult, a male. The river was still sweeping by too quickly for us to view him at our leisure, and there were no eddies. But for a short time we could see him at work, turning the logs over, browsing under them, ambling along in that nonstop way bears have of moving rapidly while appearing to be barely moving at all. He stood on his hind legs and braced himself on the roots of an uprooted tree and sniffed the air. If he smelled us, he didn't seem too concerned, dropping once again to all fours and rooting away some more.

After a few hours' float, we stopped for lunch at the base of a cliff on the right, with unimpeded views in every direction. The river was curving a bit to the north, which opened up the vista back toward the lake while pre-serving the remarkable sight of Dirst Creek. Some of the peaks around us looked like the rotten teeth of giants, as though we'd drifted into an epic. Everything around was exquisite.

Except the *Oyster Dunny*. As I sat on the gravel bar, with this incred-ible world before me, my view was marred by just one thing: the sight of a flaccid raft. The raft seemed to be deflating even while I watched. We had pumped it up before launching, and now the *Oyster Dunny* was melting, a slow-motion version of the Wicked Witch of the West's lament at the end of the *Wizard of Oz*, "I'm melting, I'm melting."

Despite the raft, we made about fifteen miles that day, running with the breeze off the Dirst Creek glaciers. Somewhere, Piggly Creek then Ugly Creek entered the river, although I couldn't tell if it was ugly or not, since I didn't see either of them. We passed a huge bald eagle nest in a standing snag and an eagle nearby being pestered by a hawk. In late afternoon the river ran for a straight stretch, and we could see, at the end of it, what we took to be Mt. Barrington.

Just before we stopped for the night, we saw another bear—this one a grizzly—working his way in and out of the edges of the forest on the left. Shortly after that, we came upon a fine little gravel bar on the same side, cut off by a thin channel running behind it. It was an intimate little location, with large views, in this case of a bluff across the channel, at the top of which I kept expecting to see a wolf or the grizzly appear at any moment, and upriver, hanging glaciers and snowfields.

That evening as we lay in the gravel at our home, I asked, "When did we last hear or see anyone?"

Max had to stop and think. "When the pilot left us up at the lake," he reminded me.

"Yeah, that's right. How many days has it been? Six?"

Max counted on his fingers. "Yep, six." He shook his head. "Hard to be anywhere for six days and not see people, isn't it? What's the longest you've gone?"

"Twelve days," I said right away. "On the Noatak, the first time I went down there in seventy-eight. I saw a float plane on a pond way off in the distance once, but that was the only sign of anybody or anything."

The evening was spectacular again, and we were in danger of becoming inured to the drama of the spectacle. There were so many impressive mountains that this sky full of peaks seemed ridiculous, a superfluity of alpine splendor. We returned to a question I'd posed to Max back at Chutine Lake, while we were paddling up the lake.

"Why do we come out here?" Max said, repeating my question.

"Right. Not just here, but why do we try to get to places like this, places that take so much time and energy and too much money?"

Max thought and paddled, then thought some more. "Well, there's the obvious: we like it, right?"

I thought of possible qualifiers, but generally this seemed right. "Yeah, sure we do."

"So then the question is, why do we like it, or what do we like about it?"

"That's it." I was beginning to feel like one of Socrates' antagonists, whose job it is to say, "Yes, Socrates," "Good point, Socrates," "You must be right, Socrates."

Max didn't say anything for a while. "So, do you have an answer," he said, "or are you waiting for me to tell you?"

"I was hoping you knew."

"Maybe we'll find out," he said, and we'd left the question there.

Now along the banks of the Chutine we came back to it. "Maybe to prove something?" Max suggested.

"Nah. Maybe when I was nineteen, but not anymore. Besides, no one cares, either. I mean, no one is paying us to do this, and we're wasting a lot of time out here when we could be improving our professional lives."

Max thought for a moment. "It's unpredictable." He waved his hand. "Everything," he said, "every part of our day is. That's what we like."

Of course he was right. There were certain things we could expect each day—the same coffee, the same oatmeal, the same arguments—but nothing else was certain. "Yeah," I said. "It's a pleasure just because we don't know what to expect, but what we get is usually lovely. Another thing," I added. "I've always felt as though being in these places, having these little adventures, improves my character—"

"Which could use it," Max interrupted gleefully.

"Ho ho. Improves my character; yours is probably hopeless."

We stared at the fire some more, entranced by the mutability of the flames, like mice by a snake. I was thinking about the despair I'd felt up at the Chutine, the despair I often feel when I first get into a wild place, and wondering why, if I am drawn to these places, that despair exists. I knew the answer: it takes a large soul to handle wildness, and my soul isn't large enough at first to match the grand things I am surrounded by. My soul is shriveled by ordinary life, and until it enlarges I can't deal with what I find in front of me. It never gets very large, only large enough to accept wild places.

⌇

We got an uncharacteristically early start the next morning, after inflating the soggy and uninspiring *Oyster Dunny*. We had camped as close as possible to where we thought we would begin our ascent of Mt. Barrington. We turned a bend or two, trying to decide where to land. We found a slough coming in from the left and, assuming that this would get us closest to the main shore, paddled, pushed, and pulled the *Dunny* up it. Max was in charge of climbing, so he selected and packed the gear we would bring: a rope, many carabiners, some slings, and two ice axes and helmets. When we were loaded, we set off through the thick growth near the slough.

Unlike more generous hills and mountains, which slope gently to greet you, Mt. Barrington was thorny and severe. There was the river plain, and there was mountain, with nothing in between to join one to the other. Peering up, we could see only scree slopes and crumbling rock noses jutting from the face; beyond that was a row of trees that we couldn't see past. We looked up and down the skirt of the mountain for a place to start. There was no good place, only places that were less impossible than others. Some of the ridges were fractured rock, and others were crumbling stone, mixed with steep scree piles. Those scree piles looked to be the only way; the other rock was too rotten and crumbly for us. I'd been hoping for granite—granite is majestic; scree, plebeian.

Walking on scree is like climbing a stream of stone. The stream flowed under us, causing a modest roar like a wave retreating from a steep and pebbly beach. Max led, and I, following, wore a rock helmet to guard against the tons of rock Max kicked down. Sometimes Max kicked a bigger one loose, and once, when he had gotten ten or fifteen yards ahead, he set free a bowling ball that came at me in such a way that I couldn't move left or right in time. All I could do was spread my legs and crouch a little, and the rock bounced through, sparing my groin.

We climbed up the first scree pile, found a nose of rock that was climbable, and went up that. This was the way to go: up or across scree, then onto relatively sturdy rock, which hadn't crumbled yet, at least until we stepped on it—then it did. The slope increased as we climbed. The traverses over the semisolid rock became more unnerving, as they dropped off sharply on either side, with hardly any good hand- or footholds. Which is where the ice axes came in. They made great poles while climbing and even better brakes when we started to slide. Max showed me how to stop my slide by digging the point of the axe into the soft ground and leaning on the handle with my chest, forcing the point deeper.

Above us was tree line, which was where this ridiculous rock swimming would end, the slope would gentle, and the ground would be firm, held together by vegetation. But that was ahead, and as the morning beat on, the climbing got harder. We never reached a point where we had to rope up, for we were more in danger of rock slides than we were of falling, although several times one or the other of us went into a slide of a dozen feet that bordered on being uncontrollable.

After about three hours we made it to the trees. We stopped to give twitching muscles a break, as our thighs spasmed. "How you doing?" Max asked.

I put my hand on my thigh. "I can feel the muscles jumping," I said. "I guess I could be in better shape for this."

We started uphill again. Laboring through a pile of branches, blow-downs, brush, we couldn't fall, but our progress was almost as slow as before. Ahead was a flat ridge, and from there we would be able to see what lay ahead.

Huffing, bleeding from small scratches, we arrived at the ridge. It was a smooth brow, very level, and behind it was a dense forest that dropped away cleanly into a bowl, at the base of which was an exactly round, blue lake. The lake was way down, and the slopes leading to it were evenly forested, with no apparent break in the trees marching down the hill.

Where we stood formed one wall of the bowl, about a quarter of it; directly across the bowl was a ridge of similar height; to the right of us, or southwest, was a lower ridge, which descended so low that there might have been an outlet stream that I couldn't see; and the fourth quarter of the bowl, on the northwestern edge, was Mt. Barrington.

From below, the ridge had appeared to be about a third of the way up the mountain. Now we could see that we were less than a quarter of the way. To get to the main mountain, we would have to descend our ridge to the left, or west, dropping a long way down onto another ridge, then ascend a steep, crumbling slope that presented one steady angle going up, without any pause in it until it came to fractured, naked rock that would be too steep to climb without ropes. It was nearly another four thousand feet, over more difficult ground than we'd already attempted; clearly this was a climb that would take a full day and maybe even then would require a bivouac somewhere on the way up or down.

We flopped in the soft bushes at the edge of the ridge and satisfied ourselves with the spectacle up and down the Chutine drainage and even over and across into the Stikine drainage. In this country, rising up a hundred feet changes one's perspective entirely. And being up a half mile, as we were, takes one into a different world. Above the riverside trees, seeing into the canyons we had passed along the way, we tried to sate ourselves with looking, and the old saw about drinking in views seemed accurate, as though we were drinking something we couldn't get enough of. It is the Mt. Olympus perspective, from the throne room of the gods.

We were directly across from the alluvial fan made by the mouth of a large tributary, Pendant Creek. The fan would make a great camp, with a broad field of gravel, with clearer water than the glacial milk of the Chutine, and with plenty of good firewood. Now we saw two moose, a cow and calf, trotting down the Pendant Creek fan, in that loping but efficient pace moose have on level ground. They seemed to be running away from something, although we didn't see any pursuit. The pair trotted to the banks of the Pendant, waded across it, then kept on to the Chutine itself, where they plunged in.

I'd never seen this before: as the two moose swam across the river, the cow swam circles around the calf, keeping it swimming in the proper direction—planet and orbiting moon of calf and mother moose, making their way through the milky waters. We watched this example of parental care, silently.

While Max rested, I wandered around our ridge, trying to take in as much of Mt. Barrington as I could. It was an odd-looking mountain, with huge bare patches of rock and smooth sides—more moonscape than mountain and not at all like most of the mountains in the rest of the range. It showed the sharp straight edge of a glacier having passed across it and hadn't ever gotten enough topsoil to hold trees to its flanks.

It was easy to imagine the mountain as a metaphor for Sid: both of them stern and rugged. It was the first time I'd ever been on a mountain named for an ancestor, and I basked both in the sun and in the dimly reflected glory of the honor. I reminded Max of that, but he wasn't impressed.

I was a little disappointed by not making it to the top, although not too much. I was here for the rivers, something I'd realized once we'd started floating. Since climbing the mountain didn't have to be done, we wouldn't do it. Besides, Sid hadn't been a mountain climber.

I looked over the valley we had come through, where the river looped like a dropped rope. I could still make out the scalloped edges of the valley of Dirst Creek off in the distance. Dirst was the angle of an "L": we were at the end of the horizontal part of the base; at the lake, we'd been at the top of the vertical leg. This would be the last we could see of Dirst: another corner or two on the river and it would be gone from sight. I was grateful to Sid and his mountain, for being the reasons I was in such a place—without them, I wouldn't be there, and that would have been a loss.

Then I joined Max lolling in the pleasant sun and the spongy moss on the slope of our ridge. For some reason I was moved to tell Max a joke. It involves three pregnant women in an obstetrician's office. One is convinced that she's going to have a girl because she was on top of her husband during conception. Another is convinced that she will have a boy, since her husband was on top. The third breaks into tears: "Oh no, I'm going to have a puppy," she laments.

We laughed and laughed at this rude joke. I laughed so hard, I squeezed tears from my eyes, and Max rocked back and forth, as though in the grip of a frenzy. When the laughter died, laughter which echoed strangely in this noisy-silent place of wind and the muted sound of the river, we still giggled for a bit.

"A puppy," Max said. "That's a good one."

Then we were quiet. Somehow we were friends now. It was as clear as anything, although I couldn't say why it had happened. It might have been the joke or the scramble up, but perhaps it was giving up on going farther. There is something unifying about failure—we had failed to make the peak, had barely tried, and now we were laughing, both at the joke and at ourselves. Before, we had been tense; after, we were pals.

Then we descended Sid's mountain. Back through the brush pile, cutting our hands and arms some more, back to the head of the rock-and-scree slope, which now looked vertical. At the top of the rock pile, it was impossible to tell which way we had come up. All routes looked more or less alike. We traversed the top of this stretch, searching for the way we had come or at least for a way that looked like less trouble. They all seemed impossible, far too steep for safety, and we were in no mood to rope up, so we kept searching. We couldn't agree on which was the way we had come, so finally we just guessed at where the raft was and took the most direct route toward it.

Stepping down into scree was worse than stepping up into it—every move threatened to break loose an avalanche of rock. We had to keep several yards away from each other to avoid being in the path of the other one's avalanche. Each step became a nearly uncontrollable slide, and each scree pile ended in a rock overhang, which we could easily slide past, into space.

The slope narrowed into the tight ravines we had come up earlier, and now we had to go single file. But we were too tired and thirsty to be very careful anymore, so one or the other was always kicking rocks down on the one below. Since Max was leading most of the time, it was me who was doing the kicking, and Max began glaring at me with a look that was a bit beyond exasperation. I kicked loose a few large boulders, which always missed Max. After a while he got used to this. "Call out, would you?" is all he asked.

When we were just about off the mountain, we came into an unfamiliar bowl of boulders just above the trees near the river. We were lost. We couldn't see the raft in either direction: not upstream, not down.

I had begun to have near-hallucinations of beer, alternating with one of ice-cold river water, so cold it would hurt to swallow. We sat for a minute on the rocks, trying to think up ways to blame the other for our mistake. We set off in opposite directions, each of us too irritated to discuss a plan of action. I walked uphill into the bowl, hoping to spot a landmark, and Max went upstream, convinced that was where the raft was. Unfortunately he was right. The place we had started from was upriver a hundred yards or so, behind a spur of rock that had blocked our view.

We wanted to camp at the broad fan of Pendant Creek we'd seen from above. Halfway across the Chutine, we stopped paddling for a few seconds to take hurried, huge gulps of the river. It was as cold as I had imagined it, but the glacial milk in it was unsatisfying, like starting to down a frosty beer that has sand. It was cold, and it eased my thirst, but it wasn't the grand, life-affirming experience I had hoped it would be.

Cutting across the racing river at an angle, we blasted into shore, then scrambled out and clung desperately to the raft, which was being torn from us. We both were so sore and tired in camp that we moved like old men, bent over, hobbling as we walked, and flopping down when we sat, unwilling to move again. We fumbled through a meal, just in time for a strong wind to come up, then some rain, and it was twenty degrees colder all at once.

I lay back against one of the bare logs that seemed to be following us from camp to camp, and I looked at Mt. Barrington. No sense of Sid came to me, nothing but an appreciation for the place I was in. Sitting at the confluence of the Pendant and Chutine rivers, I felt that if I had made it to the top of the mountain then I would have known something about Sid, and perhaps it would be true. Mountain tops are where the truth is given and received, I thought, not in valleys; so how can I know anything when I am down here instead of up there? I was down here and didn't know anything, so if I'd made it up there perhaps I would, I reasoned. It was a gloomy thought, so I crawled away from the log, and the next morning, I didn't remember how I'd gotten into my bag.

The Stikine River is a long blade of water, carving a half circle from high up on the Spatzizi Plateau in central British Columbia down to salt water at Wrangell Sound in southeastern Alaska. It comes out of a tiny lake between Mt. Thule and Mt. Umbach, just north of the 57th parallel, then flows north and west into Tuaton Lake, then as a creek into Laslui Lake, before it begins its free flow.

The Stikine runs through an almost desertlike plateau, cuts a nearly impassable canyon (the Grand Canyon of the Stikine), then enters into the open for a short time inside of the Coast Mountains that separate British Columbia from Alaska, where the only communities are those of Telegraph Creek and the ghost town of Glenora. By the time the Stikine hits Telegraph Creek, it has passed under two modest roads, including Route 37, which runs from southern B.C. and connects to the Alaska Highway in the north. Then it starts its 162-mile toboggan ride to the sea, running mostly south and west until it broadens, slows, and slumps into Wrangell Sound.

The Stikine links the homeland of two native clans, the Tlingits on the coast and the Tahltans of the interior. Early European visitors to the Stikine were probably mostly trappers and solo gold seekers until 1861, when word of a strike at Buck's Bar, near the Tahltan village below the Grand Canyon of the Stikine, prompted the first steam-powered craft to venture upstream.

One of the first published accounts of the Stikine was John Muir's. His popular dog story "Stickeen" invokes the name of the river, but more relevant is his description of a trip he made in 1879. Muir was profligate in his praise about any wild place, including the Stikine. His remark that the Stikine was a "Yosemite one hundred miles long" is often quoted, except that what he actually wrote is "[the Stikine] sweeps across [the Coast Range] through a magnificent cañon three thousand to five thousand feet deep, and more than a hundred miles long. The majestic cliffs and mountains forming the cañon-walls display endless variety of form and sculpture, and are wonderfully adorned and enlivened with glaciers and waterfalls, while throughout almost its whole extent the floor is a flowery landscape garden, like Yosemite."

Having worn out the Yukon and its tributaries and exhausted the Susitna, Sid might have been in a bit of a panic: after all, the number of navigable rivers is finite, and if you're a river man you need a river—the right one. Sid was forty-one: a perfect time for a crisis. He chose the Stikine. There was the Skeena farther south and the Frazer, but these are Canadian rivers, and that might have made a difference to a Washingtonian. And perhaps he was attracted by the Stikine's reputation for swift water. It was supposedly the fastest navigable river in North America, and the thousand-foot drop in elevation between Telegraph Creek, the head of navigation, and Wrangell on the coast made it "a navigational nightmare."

Or maybe it was the river's reputation for beauty, for the splendors of her canyon. "She's the only river that has ever held me," Sid said to Willoughby in 1928. "This old Stikine—she's a child of glaciers."

There were other reasons: a reporter wrote that the Barringtons chose the Stikine, "where river-freighting seemed likely to last longer; where, in other words, there seemed to be less chance of road or railroad interfering with water transport." There was freight to be delivered to Telegraph Creek; there were supplies to be hauled to a few ranches and to the miners and mining companies operating along the river; and there was gold, since Sid would always be a fool for gold, one of those people for whom the mineral is magic, even in small quantities, even as only an idea.

In 1916 a generation of young men was being butchered in fields throughout Europe, and radical innovations were being made in music and art, literature and science. In this context, the events on a remote, rarely traveled wilderness river were tiny. Except that here was another example of the new in conflict with the old.

The story goes that Sid showed up in Wrangell during the 1916 season and eyed the only commercial vessel on the river, an old steamboat, the *Port Simpson*. He bet all takers that he would beat the *Port Simpson* up to Telegraph Creek, and not only that, he would collect the mail and have it back in Wrangell before the *Simpson* even reached Telegraph Creek. The bet was further spiced by the fact that the *Simpson* had already left for the river, and Sid couldn't even get a pilot to point him toward the mouth of the Stikine, since he was naturally taken to be a usurper.

Of course he did find the river and won the bet. The steamboat era on the river ended when the *Port Simpson* was withdrawn from the Stikine because it was "too expensive to operate." At least, that's what they said.

By 1917 submarines were stalking ships in the Atlantic for the first time, Stravinsky had outraged Paris, Picasso was working through Cubism. And Sid was the only riverboat pilot on the Stikine.

First sounds. River: a rush, a trilling that has been there all along, but only awake do I hear and comment on it to myself. Wind: a brush against the sides of the tent, nylon against nylon, a sighing in the trees up the canyon. First smells. Of the river, not quite sharp, a richer smell than that; of the air when I stick my head out of the tent, the cleanest smell in the world—like pure oxygen mixed with pine.

In the morning I wasn't unusually sore and felt no older than usual. I had dreaded morning, sure I would find that the climb of the day before had crippled me, in a way that when I was younger wouldn't have happened. I was pleased to find myself whole.

We were going to make the Stikine that day. We had about eleven or twelve miles to run until the confluence and a few more miles to the Dokdaon. The plane was going to meet us there two days later, we hoped.

Travel by river doesn't seem as though it would be strenuous, and it isn't, not in comparison to mountaineering or hard hiking or snow camping. The wearing parts are the packing and unpacking, the setting up of camps, the rigging of the boat. Breaks are needed, layover days. Rivers keep on moving—"other waters and yet others go ever flowing on," said Heraclitus—and if you don't pause occasionally to alter the tempo of the journey, you end up feeling as though it all passed away in front of you, and you never entered it. Hence, layover days.

The champion of all layover days took place on the Rogue, in 1974, when the outfitter I guided for had a group of lawyers and district attorneys from the Bay Area. There were about twenty-four of them, equal numbers of men and women. At the put-in at Almeda Bar, downstream from Grants Pass, they walked down the ramp taking off their clothes. Almost all of them were naked by the time we pushed off, and most of them were stoned by midday. We soon realized these middle-aged professionals were determined to make this an orgy, a bacchanal.

The other guides were Brent and Bruce, two of my best friends from the early days, and a younger guide, Brad Armstrong, who died years later while climbing a volcano. We quickly entered into the spirit of things: we got naked right away, and since we were usually stoned a lot anyhow, we just started earlier in the day and were less discreet among these people. It was the first season most of us had run the Rogue, so we assumed this was normal behavior. It was a wild time, and Brent, as the lead guide, tried to keep things under control by insisting that people put their clothes on when we passed other trips. That was about the best he could do.

By the third day the libidinous lawyers had begun to slow down, as sunburns on rarely exposed places set in. This only led to further weirdness, when forms of minimal protection were fashioned, such as two bandanas tied together to form a crotch protector or bras worn without anything else.

On the fourth day we were ready for a break, having cut a wide and rude swath down the normally temperate Rogue. So we rested, down in the Rogue Flats, an area where the river finally straightens and the canyon spreads out. The guides drew lots on that fourth morning. The deal was this: whoever won got the day off, and whoever lost had to stay with the passengers all day. Some of the novelty had faded; personality flaws had been exposed along with the flesh. Plus, it was hard work keeping this group in line. They were an unruly and wayward bunch for officers of the court. The winners had to cook breakfast but then could take off, returning only to deal with dinner.

Bruce and I won, so after breakfast we prepared for our glorious day. We rigged a way to carry a jug of wine, split a tab of LSD, and headed off, naked, with some pot in a little inflatable canoe to Fall Creek, a cold fresh creek on the south side of the river that forms a series of waterfalls on its way down the canyon wall.

It was late morning when we left, paddling lazily in the canoe. As we paddled we were passed by a drift boat, an aluminum fishing boat, usually rowed by locals, that has been used on the Rogue since long before rafts arrived. The boats are high-bowed and stately, and they always seemed dignified, and the people in them seemed dignified as well, perhaps because of fishing so relentlessly.

The drift boat floated past, and we waved and said, "Hi," cheerfully oblivious to the picture we made—both of us naked, me with a braided rope of hair down my back and a long, feathered earring flapping in the breeze. I expect to cringe at this image for the rest of my life: our utter obtuseness about how we looked to others.

When Bruce and I arrived at tiny Fall Creek and were storing our inflatable and arranging ourselves for the hike, we were surprised by a drawled greeting: "Say there, boys, can I have a word with you?"

We turned to find the guide from the drift boat coming up the shore. He was a big, stocky man, wearing khaki shorts and a loud Hawaiian shirt.

"Sure," we said in unison, while Bruce stuffed the dope he had just pulled out of his ammo box back in and I was suddenly aware that the world wasn't quite as mellow a place as I'd imagined ten minutes before.

"You boys know it's illegal to be naked out here?" he asked us when he got close.

Technically we weren't naked, since we wore tennis shoes.

"Why, no, we sure didn't," said Bruce with just the right touch of concern in his voice. Bruce was five years older than me and had already done time in a federal prison for selling heroin in Vietnam, so I let him answer. I had to marvel at his technique. It is hard to discuss your own nudity calmly with a clothed, somewhat threatening person.

"Are you the guys running that nudey trip?" the man asked, switching subjects on us.

Bruce avoided taking credit: "Well, we're running a trip," he admitted, "but it's not a nudist trip. Exactly."

"I tell you what; I'm a deputy sheriff in this county, and I don't like what I'm seeing."

Bad news. The Rogue runs through two counties, Josephine and Curry. Josephine was the hipper county, which allowed hitchhiking on the freeways and had lots of alternative types. Curry, however, used to be notoriously redneck. And at the moment we were in Curry County.

"Gosh," Bruce responded after a moment, "we're sorry about that. We didn't know it was illegal. We see people without clothes all the time on the river" (which was true but at the moment irrelevant). "We'll mention it when we get back to our group," he said. "They're all district attorneys, and when we tell them it's against the law they'll straighten up."

A stroke of genius! Disgust passed over the deputy's face at the thought of lawyers, at the knowledge he had been trumped. He tried a different tack. "I've got two old folks in my boat. How do you think they like seeing you fools running around without your clothes on?"

"That's a point," I agreed. I felt brave enough now to join in. "We hadn't thought about that."

"Well, I'd better not catch you out here again," he said, turning away.

"We'll tell the others," Bruce added as the deputy made his way through the brush—a last stab at cooperation.

"Be sure you do," he called back, roughly, and disappeared past a huge fern.

Ignoring our promise, we gathered our gear and headed up the creek. To ascend beyond the first level of Fall Creek, we had to shinny up a wet tree that had fallen from the upper level down to the lower. The spray from the creek coated the tree over the years, so it had a permanent greasy patina to it, making it hard to hold on to. It angled above the rocks of the creek by twenty feet or more—a fall would hurt. We went up the tree one at a time, clinging to it with the remains of our concentration, before that ability was lost in the abyss of LSD. We slid, teetered off to one side, but kept on, until we were at the top.

And that is the last thing I remember in any order. Time fractured after that and didn't come back together until much later. All I have is images, nothing so tidy as a narrative. The bowl we climbed to was a small amphitheatre. Dividing it in two was the creek, which fell in a thin waterfall at least a hundred feet from the top of the cliff. At the bottom of the falls' plunge was a jumble of rocks that had peeled off the cliff face over the centuries. The creek fell onto those rocks and splintered into something between a spray and a mist. The recesses of the amphitheatre, behind the falls, were covered with delicate ferns and mosses and tiny, moisture-rich and sunlight-deprived flowers.

The entire plateau was wet from mist, except for the extreme edges, which rose up in a gradual slope that ended at a ridge that was the top of the falls. Climbing up the falls was impossible, although some old-time guides from another company, on a drug-induced expedition like our own, had tried it; one of them had fallen a long ways onto the rocks and had broken himself, and the others had to carry him down the slippery log and out of the canyon.

Bruce and I spent the time — and how long it was I couldn't say; all I know is that we left in late afternoon — wandering around the amphitheatre, trying to climb as high as we could on the soaking-wet face or on the dry outer walls. Each of us moved independently of the other, like random atoms in a vacuum. Sometimes we would cross each other's path and sit for a minute in silence, then say a word or two, in response to which the other might groan or burst into laughter, then we would wander on.

I remember lying on my back, my feet pointing away from the waterfall and my head thrown back so far that I was looking straight up at the falls, and at the ribbon of water swaying in the breeze, sometimes twisting around in a gorgeous sinuous pattern. When I finally sat up, I found Bruce next to me, doing the same thing.

I climbed up the face of the falls, and stopped not because I was afraid of falling — I had managed to work myself all the way up to the underside of the overhang that made the first few feet of the falls — but because I was troubled by the damage to the ferns, sentient beings that I had stepped on in my climb. Climbing down was painful, as I tried to avoid hurting their feelings.

Eventually, because of some burst of responsibility or because we were starting to lose the high, we started our descent, both literal and metaphoric. This was a fall, a postlapsarian moment, descending from the empyrean heights, Delphi, back to the dross of daily life — to other people, manmade objects, and the seedy, seamy vitality of our group. Ours was not a happy descent, for we had spent a nearly flawless few hours, once we'd escaped the deputy. I would be ashamed, later, that this perfect moment involved drugs, especially LSD. But still, it was a few hours spent in immediate contact with that little part of the planet.

We struggled down the slippery log and out through the brush to the river. We found the canoe, piled our naked selves into it, and drifted off. Only when we reached camp did we come alive, long enough to paddle into shore, to the hoots of our clan of bacchanalian lawyers and the disgusted

looks of Brent and Brad, who had been forced to deal with the lot of them
for the day.

The only other thing I recall is the scene after dinner, this last night on
the river, when the camp turned into a riot of drunk people, roaring people,
wounded people. The representative image is of two men, one of whom
might have been me, standing on a food table, screaming the lyrics from
some obscure rock song, until the table fell over, and the two people and
the rest of the wine tipped into the sand, mingling in a heap, which we then
had to clean up by flashlight.

The trip was infamous in the river community and nearly cost the outfitters for whom I worked their permit on the river. Its legend still lives on
among professional river guides. Whenever I think of it now, I am both
amused and chagrined, in equal measure, by the memory.

———

Once Max and I set out from Pendant Creek, we were carried for an hour
on a long, straight stretch, until we came to another place I'd wanted to
visit, the Barrington River. The river came in on the left, charging out of a
draw between the flanks of Barrington Mountain and Isolation Mountain.
It ran milky, like all of the other side streams.

Sid had begun mining here, on what was then called the First North Fork
of Clearwater Creek, in 1934. I once saw a picture of him and his sister,
Sibella, both in their late sixties, working a placer claim up the Barrington
in the 1940s. Even in a snapshot they seemed to be tottering. Sid swore he
took $100,000 from the claim.

At first it was a depressing stop. Earlier in the morning we had fallen
into another of our self-flagellating conversations. It was Max's turn to be
a wimp, to want to get off the river. His divorce had become final recently,
and he had taken up with a Russian émigré living in Nelson, a college town
in southern British Columbia. His sons were in transit from their mother in
South Carolina to a new home with Max and the émigré in this place they
had never been, to a demistepmother they had never seen, and Max didn't
know how any of this would go, let alone what he would do for work. For
good reason he was anxious.

I strolled around while Max fished, and as I wandered I thought of how
Sid had wandered here, too, and that this water, even these rocks, were in

some sense familiar to him. I picked up the stones. Like all river stones, these came in an infinity of shapes, with colors that were flat until I held them in the water. Then they glowed, as though the water had released some chemical, sprouting a million different colors.

I mentally assigned them. One for Sid's nephew, Billy Barrington of Anchorage, whom I had met once in 1985; another for a nephew of mine, Stevie; another for the new baby; others for Emma and Brendan, my stepchildren. As I picked up each stone and gave it a home, I thought of the connection I was making, between Sid through a rock to the recipient of it. No one would care, I was sure, but they would have to take my damn rocks whether they wanted to or not.

Finally I had a couple handfuls, and when I was done with my rock picking, I felt entirely different. The journey made sense again. There could hardly be a slighter ambition in the universe than to touch the same stones that one's first cousin thrice removed had touched. I didn't care; these were beautiful stones beside a beautiful river in a beautiful place, and Sid had led me to them. That was enough of an ambition for me.

When we left the Barrington, we were only five or six miles above the Stikine, and the braiding and islands upstream had surrendered geomorphically to one channel. Having picked up the waters of Dirst Creek and Triumph Creek, and Piggly and Ugly, and Pendant Creek and Barrington River, we were riding now on a significant river. The Chutine was rushing to meet the Stikine, and the consequence of this was waves, lots of waves. The waves came over the bow and the sides as we slopped along, undulating in that way river rafts do. You don't cut crisply through waves in a raft, even in a fully inflated one; you roll over them.

The waves kept getting bigger. We rode on the crests, mostly, but the biggest ones spilled over onto us. We would turn a corner, and Max would look at me and say, "This looks interesting," in a way that meant, "This is bigger than I thought we'd see; you didn't tell me about this; are you sure this is okay?" It was amusing the first few times.

The Chutine was still gathering volume from side streams, so the waves got taller at each new turn. Gradually the river shifted to the east, then south, and just when the waves were nice roller coasters that lifted us high and dropped us, they ended. As the confluence with the Stikine began, the river braided, spreading out into a delta of low gravel bars. The Chutine ripped along, now flowing among small islands, tearing off into one direction then another. Sometimes the channel we followed seemed to be going uphill; then it flowed to our right again, downstream. Several times I thought we had arrived at the Stikine, only to find that the water rushing in from our left was still a branch of the Chutine.

I don't think I have ever been at a confluence that was more secret. I couldn't tell where it was, when it had happened. We were on an assortment of waters, currents were mixing and twisting, and it was impossible to tell whose were whose. Somewhere in here was the Stikine.

Suddenly I knew. The mixing of currents ended, the *Dunny* was no longer being pulled in different directions, and the color of the water changed to a browner version of gray. This was open country, where the confluence of two large drainages came together and for the moment the mountains stepped back, gave way before the waters. I was exposed, open to the sky and the canyon and the big river, Sid's river, the Stikine.

BOOK II *Stikine*

One look through the raging chute that cut off the point convinced her that no man, not even Revelry Bourne, had nerve enough to plunge his ship between those close-set rocks that blocked the entrance to the short channel. There wasn't room. She was sinking to the settee with a sigh of resignation and defeat, when Bourne assumed a stance at the wheel that brought her upright again.

There was something dynamic, portentous, in the way his hands gripped the spokes. She saw his shoulders heave to a quick, strong pull. Gears screeched. The bow swung toward the Gateposts.

—Barrett Willoughby, *River House*

6   Confluence

The Stikine was a protean country—a land of breath-taking loveliness;
a land of knife-sharp cruelty.
  —Barrett Willoughby, *River House*

Sooner or later we all become who we will be. No longer are we in the process of becoming; we have become. For the rest of his days, Sid would be a Stikine river man, never running any other river but it and one of its tributaries, the Iskut. After nearly two decades of muscling his way up and down any moving water that would hold a riverboat, he settled onto the Stikine like a heron splashing onto a pond it intends to make its own.

Wrangell Sentinel, September 3, 1917: "The publisher of the Sentinel returned on the Hazel B. III Saturday afternoon from the most scenic trip he had ever taken in his life. It is needless to say that he had been to Telegraph Creek.

". . . when one is skimming along the Stikine on the scientifically constructed river boat, Hazel B. III, one is on speaking terms with mountains and glaciers. None of the detail is lost through the haze of distance. The river itself winds like a mountain trail through narrow gorges and around the bases of peaks whose summits are clad in snows eternal. The various peaks become familiar in their general appearance, but are never seen just the same twice, and are always pleasing to the eye. . . .

"The people of Telegraph Creek may not all agree on questions of politics or religion, but there is one thing on which they stand as a unit. They all swear by the Hazel B. III. They look upon Captain Sid Barrington as a public benefactor. . . .

"To recapitulate: The trip was a great one, the little boat a wonder, the skipper a prince."

———

Everything changed. The Chutine had been intimate, a river only about twenty-five yards wide; the Stikine was three times wider and felt domestic. People had been running up and down the Stikine with motors for years; before that, the Tlingits in their long boats, for centuries. Although I didn't expect to see anyone, here it was possible; on the Chutine I would have been shocked.

At the confluence the Stikine was big and broad and without much character, and the landscape seemed dull, and we felt the same. The sun was too high and too exposed and came at us in such a way that it even dulled the river.

And there was the wind. If there had been a wind on the Chutine in the last ten miles we hadn't noticed, our attention fixed on the waves. Now the wind was coming straight up the Stikine, actually lifting a spray off the surface of the river. After paddling against it for a half hour, we pulled into shore.

We stopped on a low, sandy bank, across from a bland-looking bluff. Max didn't have much to say, as he wandered around with a studiedly unrelaxed air. He was compressed, as though wound into himself too tightly. He flopped down into a space at the base of a tree and folded his arms across his chest and was silent. I burrowed into the hollow made by the roots of a cottonwood and fell asleep for a few minutes. When I woke up I saw a weird sky—a mix of everything, including clouds and sunshine and leaves blowing and birds racing past. Long streaky clouds ribboned across the sky, stretched thin by the wind. The sky was so bright, in its sickly way, that I couldn't look at it without my sunglasses, but looking at the sky in the jaundiced light of the glasses compounded my bleak mood—keeping my eyes open was almost too depressing.

The river was dirtier (literally, full of dirt) than the Chutine, and the thought of drinking it had no appeal. After a short time on the sand, we heard the distant buzzing of an engine, then saw the plane, headed downstream from Telegraph Creek, straining against the wind. It was our first engine, our first person, our first mechanical sound in seven days, and it was not welcome. We were still out, in country that most people would find wild and unnerving, but the turn from the Chutine to the Stikine had been from the bush to something else, something less, it seemed.

We dragged ourselves up and continued on. We were only three miles above Dokdaon Creek, where I had told the pilot in Telegraph Creek to meet us. This should have been a spur to our paddling but wasn't. We paddled, but it felt useless, as each stroke propelled us only a foot forward into the wind. Every once in a while I would say, "Fucking wind," and Max would add, "Yeah," listlessly.

Slowly we came around a long, right-hand turn followed by a straight stretch, leading to the sun. Squinting, I could see a hill on the right, dropping into the river. As we got closer, I saw that the river tightened there, with some type of rapid evident where the canyon pinched the river. Just beyond that pinching would be Dokdaon Creek. I couldn't tell whether a plane could land down there or not. It looked pretty skinny.

We were in a broad, open stretch of river, better for a plane, and on our left was a long sandbank. We pulled the raft up on shore, out of the wind, and looked around for a place to put a tent, in case this was the best spot to wait for the plane.

We stretched out on the raft. "So what do you want to do?" I asked Max.

Somehow he knew exactly what I was talking about. He shrugged. "I don't know. Which way do you want to go?"

"I'm not sure," I said. "I kind of want to go over to the Sheslay, and I kind of want to head down this," meaning the Stikine. "They both work for me. Although I'll bet Sid would have headed over to the Sheslay, because it would be new water."

Max nodded as though this sounded reasonable. He sighed. "I keep thinking about all of the stuff I need to do. I mean, I've got a whole new life to make, and here I am, floating rivers in the middle of nowhere with you." He gave a weak laugh.

"I know, I know," I said, trying to sound sympathetic, "but look at it this way: even if we bust down the Stikine, we'll still be out for a week or more, and we'll have to deal with getting across Wrangell Sound. Going over to the Sheslay will be cool, and it won't take much longer."

Christ, what was I saying? The idea was to go home, to get out of here, to live up to my obligations as father and husband. Three days before, I'd been ready to bolt. Now I was thinking about interesting alternatives.

Of course, if the pilot didn't show up, that would solve the problem. We wouldn't be able to get to the Sheslay, so down the Stikine we would merrily go.

"Let's go," I said, slapping my knees as I stood up.

"Where we going?" Max asked, unmoving.

"Down to the Dokdaon—let's see if the plane can get in there."

Max got up slowly. "Okay. You're the boss." It was a grudging admission.

In a few strokes, we were at the bar upstream of Dokdaon Creek known as Jackson's Landing. It had been a homestead at one time, created by Frank "Groundhog" Jackson and his wife. Groundhog had a good story: he'd discovered a huge coalfield in British Columbia and sold it for $3 million. He went south to San Francisco with some of the money, met and married a girl, then returned to the Stikine with his bride.

We walked through a field of tall horsetail ferns, taller than our heads, along what seemed to be a trail in the direction of the creek. When the trail ended, we were at the shore of the Dokdaon.

The Dokdaon is a classic glacier-fed stream. It descends from high up in a cirque of mountains with vivid names, such as Devil's Elbow, Butterfly, and Phacops. Glaciers and permanent snowfields hunker in the mountain valleys, producing the Dokdaon and several other creeks that feed the Stikine fifty miles downstream from where we were. These mountains are the hub of a wheel; the spokes are the streams; and the wheel is the Stikine.

The creek came tearing out of the mountains in a blue-gray flood, over clean, smooth stones. Such a creek is just icy, murky water and stones. By the time it reached the Stikine, it was a powerful flume that exploded into the Stikine like the spray from a fire hose.

On the downstream side of the Dokdaon was a beach, a perfect camp with wildflowers, a grove of trees, and the view up the Dokdaon. But I had my doubts about a plane landing in here. The river was only seventy-five feet wide, maybe. The pilot wouldn't have much help downstream either, as the Stikine split in two around a big island about a quarter mile away, and to land coming upstream would mean passing over the island, dropping down quickly onto the river, and coming to a stop at the beach, before the rapid. It looked dicey, but it was also a lovely place to spend a couple of nights.

"Pretty," Max said, "but he can't land here, can he?"

"Oh shoot, that's what bush flying is all about. He'll get a kick out of it," I added. We retraced our steps to the raft, trying to catch glimpses of the rapid just above the Dokdaon as we walked. It wasn't much: a pile of boiling water, a mix of currents pulling at the tubes of the raft. We bubbled over the whirlpool, were spit out on the other side, and in a few strokes were in the long eddy caused by the confluence of the Stikine and the Dokdaon.

In August of 1986 I almost made it to the Stikine, but not quite; I got only as close as Wrangell. I had been on the Noatak River in northern Alaska running a trip with Denny Eagan, a trip that included a famous folk singer. At the end of this trip—during which I often broke into song, auditioning for the folk singer—I tried to convince Denny to go down to Wrangell with me and run the Stikine, but he had girlfriend problems in Anchorage and couldn't. I had a ticket south anyhow, so I bounced out of Anchorage down to Juneau, where I spent a few days chasing Barrington information in the state archives, then moved on to Wrangell.

I asked around about Sid, and about people who had known him, and was referred to the town clerk, the harbormaster, the manager of the wastewater plant, and a woman named Darlynn. As a result I found a man who had traveled a time or two with Sid, a riverboat Sid had piloted, and even Dar Smith, one of the deckhands who had worked for the Barringtons for many years.

The first morning I talked to George Gunderson in the kitchen of his house a few streets up from the waterfront. George was a large man in his eighties, large in the way that north-country men ought to be: tall and big-boned and solid. He had come to Wrangell for the first time in 1910 and worked fish traps for many years. He remembered taking a trip up the Stikine in 1936 or so with Sid, "just for fun." He cackled about the first night, when they tied up on shore at the Canadian border and he was assigned to keep an eye on the boat. "You watch it close," he was told; "the river'll drop and leave us high and dry if we're not careful." He stayed up most of the night, watching, and when morning came he thought he would make some coffee for the crew. Having been on salt water all his life, he was puzzled when he looked around the boat and couldn't find any freshwater on board. "For Christ's sake, what kind of outfit is this?" he remembered thinking. Then Deaf Dan McCullough, an Indian mate for the Barringtons, came along and took the water kettle out of George's hands and reached over the side of the boat to get water from the river. George remembered feeling "like a tinhorn."

George's memories were charmingly random. He remembered things twice, then parts of events, and skipped happily over decades and people without any concern for sequence or order. "Barrett Willoughby was a plump, blond girl. Hazel was kind of jealous of her; thought she spent too much time around Sid. . . . I found a gleaner once [a mix of zinc, lead, and gold in the same rock] with Sid about twenty miles up the Iskut. Damn thing was nailed to the ground, it was so heavy."

Sid and Hazel's only child, York, was killed in 1923 at the age of twenty in a hunting accident. "I remember when the boy was killed," George told me. "I got married in twenty-three. My first wife died of cancer. She [Hazel] took the boy's death awful hard. Never recovered. He and another fellow were duck hunting up on the Stikine Flats, and the other boy stubbed his toe, put a hole in the middle of York's back. Used to be a black cloud over the two of them."

I wanted to know what Sid had been like, what kind of man he'd been. George answered, in a way. "Hill was a kidder. He had his superstitions. No whistling in the pilot house. Hill was friendlier. Sid was more the businessman. Hill was Catholic; Sid was Christian Scientist. Had big arguments among themselves. Argued religion more than anything.

"I remember a funny thing Sid did once. There was a kid who worked on the boats, Daggett, or something. He had a depressed chest, and everyone said it was from him wearing a cross around his neck all the time. Daggett prayed that his chest wouldn't be caved in like that. Sid got ahold of him and said, 'You know I had a devoted mother. Every night she came down and kneeled by my bed and prayed. And yet, I'm still here!'

"Sid bought his wife lots of diamonds and rings. He had a bank account on his wife. Things got tough, he'd sell them; things got better, she got more." I liked that detail—it made Sid sound rakish and unconventional, two conditions I'd always aspired to.

"I was everything on that trip," he said, switching subjects again. "I was cook, engineer, purser, pilot-captain, night watchman, and freight handler. Paid for my trip that way." And suddenly, "I worked all morning on that shaft. It was on a universal, you know; that was the clever thing about those boats: you could lift and lower the drive shaft with a crank, for when you got to shallow water, and so the shaft had to be on a universal joint.

"Not a lot of unloading until we got to Telegraph Creek. Had to wrestle those crates and boxes. The winter supplies for the trading post. There was a Chinese cook in the store at Telegraph then. Women who had come up-river with us on the boat didn't want eggs, but moose steak. The cook was tired of cooking moose steaks; he wanted to cook some of the eggs he'd just gotten." Then, out of the blue, "Did you know Sid was the first one to take a steamboat through Miles Canyon on the Yukon?

"They hit a snag up there." (Now we were back on the Stikine in 1936.) "Blankets were waving in the snag after we hit it. Poked a hole in the window and took some blankets right out of the boat, we come so close."

George began to wind down like a mantel clock, and the distances between stories got greater, and the stories became fragments. I thanked him and went away, but I'm not sure he noticed.

I went out to see Robin Larson, the head of the Wrangell sewage plant. Robin, with wild white hair and beard, stood out among the working-class souls of Wrangell, since he looked like an aging beatnik, and that—more or less—is what he was. He had studied photography with Ansel Adams in the mid 1950s in San Francisco and had left California in 1971 because, he said, "California was destroyed, was destroying itself." I didn't disagree.

When I arrived, Robin was thumbing through a book called *Paradise North: An Alaska Year*, by Henry Barrows. It is the account of 1953, a year in which Barrows was stuck in Wrangell. "I knew Barrows had gone on the *Judith Ann*," Robin told me, "but I hadn't remembered this," and he passed the book to me. He pointed to a passage about a trip that Barrows had taken on the *Judith Ann*, which read, "Each time the skipper, Sid Barrington, with unshakeable aplomb, merely backed up a few feet, changed course slightly, and found the uncharted, unmarked channel. . . . Sid Barrington is a landmark of the North, a river man without peer. Now eighty-four years old [actually only seventy-eight in 1953], tall, lean, and tough as rawhide, he is still handling a job that would quickly exhaust both the physical and nervous energy of many young men."

I made plans with Robin to visit his boat after work, then drove into town to see Dar Smith at his daughter Darlynn's house. Dar was then eighty-six and fit, except for having Alzheimer's, his daughter told me. He was a grinner: perhaps it was the Alzheimer's, but he grinned all the time, when remembering something sad, something funny, something odd, something unpleasant. He floated from topic to topic and repeated himself and didn't have the slightest sense of what yesterday had been like, but he remembered the Barringtons and the boats well. He was as close as I was ever going to get to knowing what Sid's river life had been like; men such as George Gunderson and Dar were the only ones who could tell me.

Dar came north to work the river in 1923, the year York Barrington died, and quit twenty years later simply because "I got tired of it," he said. He didn't say what he got tired of, and I assumed it couldn't be rivers. "Tired" of not making much money, that I could understand; "tired" of not having a steady home or not being there very often, that made sense.

"I was working fourteen, fifteen hours a day during the season, and we didn't get paid until the fall. They paid us all at once, at the end of the season. I worked six or seven months, and would live on that all year. They had a bookkeeper in an office in Wrangell, right across from the Stikine Inn, Andy Smith. He was an Englishman, a chintzy one. He was always trying to cut us short. You had to watch him all the time."

Dar described himself as "a real Scotchman with money," and this, plus the fact that he didn't drink or smoke, meant that when spring came around he often had more money than the Barringtons. "I loaned Sid three or four hundred dollars several times," he recalled. "Never got a kickback on it," he added, with a laugh at their cheapness.

In April each year, Dar would come to Wrangell from Oak Harbor. In the first part of May, they'd make a trip upriver in a small boat to see what changes the winter had brought to the river, and to deliver freight to Telegraph Creek. That trip might take as long as ten days. Their next trip was with a full load in a bigger boat. After mid May they ran a trip a week.

"You had to watch what you were doing, especially on the big boat," Dar said. "You couldn't get into certain spots. Hill would run into the brush on shore sometimes and Sid would chew his hind end out. Hill got better as a pilot, but he never got half as good as Sid.

"Sometimes windows would get punched out of the boat when we drifted too close to the shore, and I remember one time looking back after we were too close and seeing some blankets that had been drying on deck hanging from tree branches behind us," a story that sounded suspiciously like George Gunderson's recollection of the trip of '36.

"The last trip of the season with the big boat was at the end of September. We'd take people from town and load the boat light. If there were too many people on board, I'd take my bag down to the freight room so some passenger could have my bunk. Last trip of all was in the first week of October with mail and perishables. A lot of folks just went for sightseeing. Ten or fifteen passengers."

Dar's role was diverse. "I was the guy that did everything," he chuckled, a claim made by George as well. "I was supposed to be the purser, but I waited tables, ran the lining cable [used to winch riverboats upstream past places where the current was too strong for the boat's engines], all that. I'd have my white coat on and be serving dinner, and Sid would start hollering at me to go run a cable. Me and Dan McCullough did all the dragging. Dan did the rowing and I handled the cable. Old Dan liked to have a drink once in a while. Then he'd start to feel real good. Sometimes he'd be in the line boat with me that way. Wish I had a nickel for every yard of cable I laid out," Dar added wistfully.

Another member of the crew was Jack Wilson, the cook. Jack worked for nearly fifteen years with the Barringtons, Dar recalled. "He'd been a rounder alright. He got stuck in some trouble somewhere and came over to our side of the border. You couldn't get a better meal than you could get on the riverboat. He was always getting written up for the food." ("Food on the boat is famous all over Alaska," says an article from *Sunset* magazine in May of 1943.) "I used to tease him, tell him they were just giving him the bull. He'd get so mad. But we were good friends. What really made him mad was that I would get more tips than he did, since I was waiting on the tables. We could serve twenty people in the galley on the bigger boats, and getting tips was Jack's thing. Jack Wilson liked his liquor. In town he'd get looped up. But he was a good-natured old guy. He's in heaven. Sometimes the engine would shake the kitchen galley. Old Jack used to rave then. Jack was an old Englishman. You could never get anything out of him. He'd never talk about his past."

Dar confirmed one of the tallest tales about Sid, gambling away the riverboat in Nome. "True story," said Dar, nodding. "Sid was a gambler alright."

Gradually Dar, like George Gunderson, faded. Sleepily he said, "They couldn't afford to fire me, because they'd have to borrow some of that money to get started every season. They weren't much for hard work," he claimed. I bristled a little at that but then remembered I wasn't much for hard work either.

"There were special spots they would tie up at," Dar muttered. "Depending on when they left Wrangell. At the Custom House, Mink Farm, Hell-Roaring Jackson's. Down at Glenora, about twelve miles below Telegraph Creek.

"Sid was about six feet tall and broad. Neither one was fat. Hill was tighter than the bark on a tree," he rambled on. "Sid's wife didn't go very often; Hill's wife didn't go at all. Harry would run a second boat if they needed it. You couldn't get into certain spots on the bigger boat. Seems like every trip there would be something odd on the trip."

His head dropped to the side. "They got mad as hell when I quit. They wouldn't raise my wages when I told them, so I quit." His eyelids fluttered. "Just quit," he said.

I had thought Dar, as a contemporary, might have worshipped at the feet of Sid, but it wasn't so. To him Sid had been an ordinary man—and why not? He was, flawed just as other men are. Yet Dar had helped me see, a little, what being on the Stikine with Sid had been like. To complete that vision, I needed a riverboat.

It was still early, so I walked from Chief Shakes Island in the center of Wrangell harbor down to the Stikine Inn near the ferry terminal, and beyond, to the wooden stairs leading to a beach with Tlingit petroglyphs. It was a glorious day, a large, epic day. The sky was so blue, it was nearly purple, with just a few soft clouds suspended in the foreground. In the distance, to the west, I could see the ridges of Etolin Island, and to the east, the glaciers of the LeConte Glacier and the huge drainage out of which the Stikine flows. At that moment I regretted not having made a trip up to Telegraph Creek, since I could tell, even from the beach, how magnificent the river would have been on a day like that. I wondered if, like Dar and George and Sid and Hill, I would ever see it.

Robin Larson had told me to drive south on the only road to where the pavement ends and to count drives until I got to his turnout. I parked and started following a trail. At the first step I plunged into a rain forest, with mosses and ferns underfoot everywhere and groundwater seeping into boot prints on the trail. After a quarter mile of this dark, drooping forest, I emerged onto a brilliantly lit beach. I had to look around for a moment, blinking, before I could see. Then my vision cleared and there was the *Judith Ann*: a boxy, rectangular block whose bottom half was painted brown, topped by a band of red, then white for the upper half. Before I noticed the wooden pad she rested on, it seemed for a moment as though she were preparing to pull away.

Robin and his companion, Cindy, showed up moments later. The boat seemed much smaller than I would have imagined, although at sixty-four feet long with a seventeen-foot beam she was about the same size as many of the *Hazel B.*'s. Robin took me on a tour of the boat while Cindy brewed coffee in the galley. First was the engine room, where six keels had been laid and the original 165-horsepower diesel engine sat. Robin was planning to replace the engine with a newer one, then take the *Judith Ann* upriver. He showed me the staterooms—tiny cubbyholes framed in plywood, three on each side—and we walked along the outside railing, looking toward the islands of the strait.

Robin bought the *Judith Ann* after seeing her sitting in Wrangell harbor, soon after he moved to town in 1971. "The tide was rushing through her," he remembered. "The boat didn't have an unbroken window at the time." He went to the bank that owned the boat (having foreclosed on a loan to the previous owners) and made a "ridiculous offer" of a thousand dollars. The bank officer agreed it was ridiculous but three months later accepted it.

I walked through the boat on my own, stopping in the main lounge, from which there was an uninterrupted view of the stunning setting. Offshore a hundred yards was a small island, where Robin had a permit for an oyster farm. Beyond that, on the far side of Zimovia Strait, was Etolin Island, heavily forested with a steep spine of mountain running through the center. Mountains and trees and islands to the south, more of each to the north.

I climbed the stairs to the upper deck and looked off the stubby, blunt bow. I could imagine the *Judith Ann* churning up a river, passing near to glaciers, sometimes drifting too close to the shore and losing blankets to the trees. I could imagine her tied up for the night, quietly lifting to the rhythm of the river, the diesels shut down and the forest still. I could even picture Sid in the pilothouse, searching out channels in the river, reading the currents as though he were reading the expressions on the face of Hazel, his absent wife.

I had a cup of coffee with Robin and Cindy, took some pictures, and savored the sight of the boat, trying to make it mean something. When I left, I paused before disappearing into the forest. Such an ordinary-looking thing. Attractive in a way but no more shapely than a shoe box, its boxiness relieved only by the solid wall of windows at the front of the upper deck. Yet still a romantic vessel, if one is inclined to see a riverboat as romantic. It had no graceful lines, no air of smooth passage or artful appeal to it. But could it float? Would it move? Then that was enough. It was a riverboat— a noble thing to be.

I left Wrangell the next morning, after an evening spent in the lounge of the Stikine Inn on the waterfront. I arrived in late afternoon and stayed until the touring Top 40 band from L.A. had set up, warmed up, and launched into the familiar bar songs, including "Proud Mary." I watched pink-and-white afternoon clouds darken, a wind sock on the wharf dangle limply in the still air, a half moon hang above it, and the heavy forest of Woronofski Island beyond glisten like the fir of a sleeping bear. There was a handprint on the inside of the window of the bar, as though someone had tried to reach out and touch the view. I listened to too many drunk people, including one woman who kept saying to anyone who entered, "Oh shit, you should have been in here earlier," for no apparent reason, since nothing had happened since the bar had opened.

Flying out of Wrangell, past the mouth of the Stikine, I looked upriver at the huge drainage and the spiny green carpet that surrounded it and the glaciers feeding it. Up there were new experiences, new waters, new visions for me. I didn't know what they would be, only that they would be worth my time.

7 *Eddy*

I see my life go drifting like a river
From change to change
  —W. B. Yeats, "Fergus and the Druid"

Max and I glided into the beach, grinding on the sand. For a moment neither of us moved—river fatigue, the pleasure of not having to paddle, of being somewhere we will stay.

We unloaded the *Oyster Dunny* and lifted it out of the river so I could repair it in the morning. We untied all of the straps and took everything out of the raft and spread it on the beach. As day ebbed, I went inside the tent. I sat in the doorway, looking out over the big eddy of the Dokdaon—eddies are rips in the fabric of the universe, powerful things, like crevasses or black holes. They attract animals to them, and people, because their whirling creates a gravitational force; at least, this is my theory—and pondered the breadth of the day. We had traveled from the base of Mt. Barrington in that other world, the Chutine basin, past the Barrington River, and out onto the Stikine, then battled the hellish wind and landed here at this powerful spot.

Dar had called this place "Hell-Roaring Jackson's," which is a name one might prefer to "Groundhog." But I could see why "Groundhog"/"Hell-Roaring" Jackson had liked it here. It is the entrance to a new geologic and climatic zone. The whirling eddy is one sort of portal; the Dokdaon is another, opening into the splendid Ambition mountain cluster. There were dramatic views downstream of a Valhalla of mountains, including, literally, Valhalla Mountain. The colors at sunset changed constantly, and the greens and whites of the mountains mixed with the pastels of the sunset, making a weirdly fractured rainbow.

I fell asleep early and woke up when Max entered the tent, having been out by the fire whittling a spoon for me, to replace one I'd left somewhere on the Chutine. One of the last things I was aware of before I drifted off again was the sound of a radio playing—not a real radio, of course, but a ghost radio, the buzzing of my injured ear making sense out of the subtle sounds it heard in the only way it could, by relating them to a familiar one: that of a radio turned so low that the song is barely distinguishable. I hadn't realized that "Red Rubber Ball" was on my ear's playlist: "The roller coaster ride we took/is nearly at an end . . ."

———

The Dokdaon was familiar terrain; I'd been here once before. In 1988, two years after I left Wrangell, I returned, and floated the Stikine from Telegraph Creek. With me was a river-guide pal, Dewi (DOW-ee) Butler—a Welshman, rock climber, ski patrolman, and prolific beer drinker.

I'd returned for the Stikine, to finally see what this river that had been Sid's river home for thirty-eight years—and about which I'd heard so much —looked like, felt like to travel. I knew it was a fast, big, beautiful river and canyon; I wanted to see how fast, how big, how beautiful.

We took ten days. It was a strange trip, to be traveling with just one raft and two people. And it was a strange river: as fast as any river I'd been on but with few rapids, so we could travel fifteen or twenty miles while floating. The Stikine was surely beautiful too.

We'd caught a flight from Wrangell to Telegraph Creek with a pilot I'd met in '86. Telegraph Creek is squeezed into a canyon that is steep and rocky on the village side, having a more gentle slope opposite. On the village side, the vegetation is sparse and thorny, mostly low juniper bushes and a few cedar trees. Across the river is a mixture of small-leaf maples, lodgepole pines, poplar, and black spruce.

There were 350 people living there, 250 of them Tahltans and the rest Anglos. The only store was the Riversong Café and general store, which also rented a few rooms. The café had tables in the front section, with cash registers and counters on both sides. Piles of goods were crammed into spaces all over the building, even hanging from the ceiling. You could get a cup of coffee, which we did, as well as a bicycle, which we didn't. There were no signs of Sid, except that everyone we talked to had heard of him.

During the first two days on the river, we left the badlands of the Telegraph Creek area behind and entered a more rolling, almost tundralike terrain. There were snowy peaks off to the east, and the worn, bare, high ridges behind us of Dodjatin Mountain. Mt. Glenora passed by, on which John Muir had a great adventure, saving the Reverend Samuel Young.

On the third day we passed the Three Sisters, famous landmarks on Sid's trips: three spires of rock, sticking straight up out of the river, fifty to seventy-five feet high, the biggest one upstream and descending in size from there. They are a medley of pebbles and crumbling stone. We dropped into the eddy behind the last one. Dewi started climbing up, holding on to a long nylon line, while I clung to the rock with my fingertips as the raft churned in the eddy. From the top of the rock, he held the bow line of the raft while I climbed to join him. It's a strange perspective, of a river from the top of a narrow rock in the center of it. I tried to picture the *Judith Ann* charging through here, drifting to the outside of the turn, and how these rocks might have looked from that view—like steaming through Stonehenge.

At the confluence with the Chutine River, twenty miles downstream of the Three Sisters, we looked to camp, but there was no inviting place to stop. It was late afternoon by the time we went by; I craned my neck to see if I could get a glimpse of Mt. Barrington, and I thought I did—craggy and foreboding?—although I couldn't say for sure.

Below the Chutine the landscape changed completely. The hills and mountains before had been rounded, and the canyon had looked like an arid, windy place; now the mountains shot straight up, angular and snow-covered, and the canyon tightened around us. Soon we came to the mouth of Dokdaon Creek. A spectacular place: the creek was shockingly blue, there was a big eddy below it for fishing, the view up Dokdaon was so glorious it made me ache, and the river had formed a broad floodplain that we could easily walk upon. Something about the spot seemed familiar, as though I'd been there before. Later I realized what it was: a photo I owned showing Sid at this same spot with two of the *Hazel B.*'s. Same river, same currents, same bluff across the way.

We floated. The only time we lifted an oar was to stay off one shore or another; otherwise the current carried us so swiftly that no downstream strokes were needed. I could see why it had been a challenge for Sid to bring his heavy boats upstream, bucking this stiff current all the way.

By the fourth day we were in between the mountains of the Sawback Range to the west, a row of 7,000-foot peaks, and the cluster of peaks in the east circling the 9,629-foot-high Ambition Mountain. No matter where we looked, there were mountains, coming into view slowly—everything appeared in this fashion, unfolding in smooth progressions, vistas revealing themselves to us in increments as we went downstream. Sharp, jagged, steep-peaked mountains and glaciers drooping from them or nestled in cirques between them. It was dazzling, constantly distracting the eye. The mountains were wooded partway up their slopes, then the trees gave way first to barren ground or slabs of granite, then to snow and ice, cornices and glaciers. Some peaks were snowcapped; others were too steep for that. The mountains seemed old—I didn't know if that was true in geologic terms, but there was nothing new about them, except the green growing things. Otherwise they seemed like the oldest beings on the planet.

We began to see huge dead trees in the river, wedged on sandbars and sticking out from shore. They looked like shipwrecks or skeletons, a graveyard of trees, thousands of trees, jammed into piles, covered in the grayish silt that the river left on them when it receded. We would come around a bend in the river and find that our river had split into a dozen channels, each channel defined by a pile of logs ten or fifteen feet high, one hundred feet long. We had heard in Telegraph Creek that a canoeist had drowned in one such pile recently, and his body had not been found. We looked for his canoe; his body we didn't want to find.

On the fifth day, we entered Little Canyon, the only thing we'd seen that resembled a true canyon. It was a tight, swift two miles, a straight shot south. It had been a major challenge for Sid because of the current, which was as fast there as at any place on the river—10 knots or more.

We entered the land of waterfalls. Several times we rowed into tiny estuaries searching for waterfalls; in one we were able to wind a quarter mile up to reach a pretty little falls cascading down, where two ducks were loitering. There were waterfalls on every side, and we would turn from our conversation once in a while to take notice of them. But mostly we gossiped about other guides and about what it was like to guide. Dewi said he liked guiding, because when he was too old and feeble to climb anymore, he could still be a river guide.

We stopped twice at large moraine drainages, the Deeker and Patmore Creek areas. Dewi caught a small salmon at Deeker while standing among thousands of bear prints. I walked a little ways up Deeker Creek, until I was maybe fifty feet above the river. Even this lifted me to where the entire Ambition Mountain range across the way was exposed, spread before me like some improbable panorama—I could have taken photos forever and never captured the largeness of it.

Dewi and I swapped river sex stories as we swept along. Tales of river guides at play: a beach on the Middle Fork renamed for a popular sex act; the time a woman came to my sleeping bag on the Tuolumne late one night with a bottle of zinfandel and a condom; a speed record for seduction, set by a guide in a cave before lunch on the first day of a trip on the Stanislaus. Dewi told a story about a guide he knew in Utah who had been trying to convince his new bride that guiding wasn't all debauchery, so he took her on a trip down the Green River, and while walking to their tent one night, they tripped over another guide and a passenger going at it.

For three days we turned a large half circle around the bundle of peaks and glaciers that center on Ambition Mountain. Cone Mountain, a rounded peak near the river and at the front of the Ambition Mountain complex, had been in view for days and would continue to be for several days more. When it was finally out of view, we would be turning around another mountain, which would have been a distant peak on the horizon a few days before, become the dominant point on the landscape for a time, then would fade, becoming one peak among many.

I pictured the foredeck of a riverboat sneaking up around the corner, preceded by the drumming of its engines, a cluster of passengers on deck looking anxiously ahead. In the wheelhouse I thought I could see a man smoking a cigar, one hand on the wheel. Then Dewi tossed a lure into the river and I was brought back to the quiet of two of us and one silent raft.

The snag graveyard was at its most pronounced where the Scud River entered in a fan. Once there must have been a flood down the Scud— some rhyming wit named three consecutive tributaries the Scud, Mud, and Flood—and as a result both sides of the Stikine were filled with standing dead trees and littered with logs. The dead trees everywhere were eerie, as though there were something unsavory about these deaths. Branches would suddenly pop up out of the water, like ghouls rising from a watery grave, then sink again.

We had stopped at the Flood River in midafternoon of our seventh day, and went for a walk up the river. I was carrying the bear gun casually in one hand. We walked about fifteen yards when suddenly there was a roaring gunshot. I flinched. Dewi jumped five feet sideways and ducked as though there were going to be more explosions. But it was only our gun, blowing off right between us, firing into the ground. We stared at each other. Dewi looked as though he were about to say either, How could you be so stupid? or, Why are you shooting at me?

Instead he demanded, "What the fuck happened?"

"The gun went off," I said, helpfully. I held it up, looking at it carefully. "I know I didn't pull the trigger. Are you hit?" I asked, although it was obvious that he wasn't.

"No," he said. "I can't fucking believe I'm not." He looked down at his leg, then searched his arms.

Dewi said he'd felt the wind from the slug whistle past his ankle. His ear hurt from the roar. I remembered Sid's son, killed while duck hunting along the Stikine. This would be a bit too ironic, if I had managed to kill Dewi while retracing Sid's life. What had the old fellow, George Gunderson, said about Hazel? "She took the boy's death awful hard. Never recovered . . ."

We found a cabin just downstream in late afternoon. There was a welcoming note tacked to a tree, encouraging people to stay, so we did. In the cabin next morning: sun coming through the cabin door, clouds that will soon burn off caught in the trees. Clean air everywhere—I felt as though I were drinking it. The mountains across the river appeared to have been snowed on. Rain had poured like a madman's tears for a while during the night—had to set up buckets to catch drips through the roof. Got a glimpse of the moon when the clouds cleared and I went out to pee. Stepping outside, peeing; cold and wet, standing exposed to air, wind, rain, smells, sounds, trying to pee as swiftly as possible; hard to do.

We lie in our bags on the floor, and soon Dewi tells a story about being in Greece with a girl hopelessly drunk on wine, then I tell one about nightclub hopping in Mexico City with a bombed Mexican river runner who wants to buy me a stripper using his credit card, and about being in Reno with only ten dollars when I needed twenty dollars' worth of gas to get to where I was going, and putting the ten bucks on one hand of blackjack, and winning.

I stepped outside and once more saw no sign of Sid. There were only mountains reaching up into the soft clouds that hadn't been pummeled by the warming sun. There was the sound of birds and of distant waterfalls, that wonderful muted roar. And the river, steaming past. So this is where Sid had spent his time—not a bad place to work. He might be flattered that I'd come all this way just because of him.

We found a tributary, Stirling Creek—I remembered what plainspoken Dar Smith had told me about Teddy Stirling, a nephew, he said, of Sid's: "Good on the wheel but never did any work. A woman-chaser. A fat slob and a gambler"—and followed it up to a little grotto where there was a twenty-foot twisting falls at the head of a pool. A smooth, clean gravel bar on one side, sheer rock walls surrounding the pool, big spruce all around, glacier-blue water, and huge peaks standing behind the falls. We stayed for a few hours in this ridiculously grand spot, scrambling through the brush and ferns to the lip of the falls, feeling its power. What pleasure there is in falling water, to feel it vibrating through the bottom of your soles.

More stories about guides we had known. About Bruce Reitherman, whose father was one of the original directors for Walt Disney, and who was the voice of Mowgli in *The Jungle Book* movie; about Tim Blythe, the strongest guide I ever knew, whom I once saw hit a man who was trying to tackle him, the blow lifting the man in the air, and when the man touched the ground he was out cold; about Jim Gloystein, who would get his fellow guides free drinks by playing piano in a saloon near the Stanislaus after trips, and where the evenings always got wild—an inspired cowboy once rode his horse into the saloon.

We tried to visit Darsmith (Dar Smith) Creek but couldn't find the mouth of it, and we kept an eye out for Jack Wilson Creek, too—named for the cook on Sid's boats—but got distracted by other things and missed it as well. We camped one night at the base of Mud Glacier, in sight of Kate's Needle—at 10,002 feet, the tallest peak along the river. Vertical and craggy and snow-covered and striking. The evening clouds were stuck on the tip of Kate's Needle. Snow had been driven into the face, etching itself into tiny crevices and ledges and the grain of the rock.

Nearing the end of the river, we hiked up to the Great Glacier, a famous place for the Stikine and for Sid. Sid would sometimes take people from Wrangell up to the Great Glacier for the day. At the glacial bay in front of the glacier, we had a fine view of both the glacier and its icebergs floating in the bay and even drifting down the exit creek, having worked their way free from their mother-bergs. The ice had different shades of blue to it. The deeper into it we could see, the bluer it was.

Rained all day, while we worked our way from the mouth of Shakes Slough to the coast, seven hours and twelve slow miles, at the end of which we passed out of the Stikine and shot into the Eastern Passage, to a Forest Service cabin at a place called Garnet Ledge. Being on the river that day was miserable, as being on a river sometimes is. Rain fell constantly, and the clouds were as low in the valley as they could get. One of us huddled in the bow, trying to stay warm, while the other rowed. There wasn't much to see, just a grim landscape of sandbars and dead trees, with a background of gray. It was like most last days of a trip by river, as you approach the end and begin to know you are leaving the world of the river, returning to that other world.

Getting to the cabin was welcome: the end of rowing, the end of being wet. The cabin had a loft and big windows facing the estuary, the grave of the Stikine. We festooned the cabin with drying clothes. There were supposed to be garnet stones in a ridge up the trail from the cabin, but when we went to look in the afternoon, we couldn't find any. Dewi took two short naps that afternoon, then surrendered to trip fatigue and went to bed. I drank lots of coffee and looked over my notes, trying to see what I had found of Sid. What had I learned? That it was a beautiful river. What else? Only that he'd been lucky to spend nearly forty years running it.

Like Dewi I fell asleep early in the hot, dry cabin. I'd be deeply asleep, then rivet awake as though there were something important I'd forgotten to do, then plunge back into sleep moments later. In the morning I noticed a garnet on a two-by-four in the cabin. Now that I knew what to look for, I went back to the ledges to see if I could find some. They were easy to spot. They seemed to be littering the ledges, in big clusters of mud and gravel and stones. I gathered a handful.

A jet boat took us across Wrangell Sound, and in Wrangell we were dropped at the airstrip in our muddy clothes. A jet arrived; we were about to board.

I had seen Sid's river, at last. It was satisfying to have finally made it, but now I was made dizzy by the speed at which we were moving away from the Stikine. Wait, I thought, am I done? Was that enough? It didn't feel like it; the Stikine had been beautiful, and interesting because of Sid, but it was Sid's, not mine. Even as we boarded the plane I said to Dewi, "Maybe one of those tributaries . . . ?"

———

The morning sun shone through the ceiling of the tent, which was filled with mosquitoes lazing drunkenly about. Max had left the mosquito netting open when he went to sleep, and the shitty little bastards got in, despite the rankness of our smell. We lay about in the overheated tent in our underwear, a disgusting sight: two middle-aged men, too hairy, too pale, and too soft for such a spectacle. While I killed mosquitoes we talked about the possibility of transferring disease from one of us to the other via this mosquito bloodletting: if Max has a blood disease, I posited, and one of these bugs bites him and ascends to the ceiling, where I with great pleasure pop him to death between my fingers, and some of Max's blood gets on one of the thousands of little cuts on my fingers, can the disease be transferred? Max thought not, but in any case the satisfaction of feeling little mosquito parts squish between my fingers was too much to resist.

This was our eighth day, a delayed day of rest. We felt no urgency to get out of the tent or even to move. As I lay there I was aware of a dream I'd had: a World Series game, in which Bert Blyleven, a curveball pitcher from the 70s and 80s, gets hammered. He is pulled from the game, and his comment to the manager as he leaves is, "You know, you can't prepare for the big one. You think you can, but you can't." The dream seemed weighty with meaning, but what meaning? It could refer to this trip, or the melanoma, or the birth of my child, or nothing at all.

When I was finally ready to leave the tent, I was hearing Eric Clapton's "Layla" in my radio ear, which, as an unbidden buzzing in the brain, wasn't bad. Then I heard a real sound, a motorized droning that I couldn't identify at first but knew must be either a motorboat or a plane. Moments later both went by—a plane flying upstream with the wind, and a silver skiff heading downstream through the swirls at Jackson's Landing. The skiff held a woman, a man, and two kids, and they waved at us without seeming surprised to find us there. It was a bit deflating to be among people again, but both vehicles were gone soon, then the sound of them. Our beach was back to what it had been, the ripple in our universe repaired.

Looking around at our beach, I tried to see if there were differences from three years before. Since it was July instead of August, the flowers on shore —honeysuckle, with bees—were thicker. And the creek seemed to flush out even harder, faster. But the mountains were still the same, still improbably tall and varied.

We spent the morning spooning up oatmeal and coffee, talking about evolution and Lamarck. We had few ambitions for the day: to clean our persons, which stank; to clean our clothes, which also stank; to repair the raft; and to break out our sole bottle of brandy.

While Max messed with the gun, I looked over the map again, so that we could make an informed decision about what to do next. That question lingered on the mild air around us. I calculated 157 miles from the Hackett-Sheslay confluence to the beginning of Taku Inlet and another 40 down the inlet to Juneau. Ten or eleven days for this. Or we could continue down the Stikine, which would mean traveling 120 miles or so to the mouth of the river, then crossing the 6 miles of open water to Wrangell Island. This wouldn't take more than six or seven days.

Then I bathed. In my more vigorous youth I had washed in frigid arctic waters, jumping in to soap up, then using a bucket of frigid water to rinse off on shore. I was never very happy about flinging myself into water so cold that it stops the heart and the brain, shrivels the scrotum, tears at the senses, but at least in my twenties I would do it. Now, I dipped myself into the very cold Stikine, getting as little of the river on me as I could, then used water heated on the fire to rinse off. This warm rinse was such a vast improvement over ice water that I marveled, again, at how stupid one can be when one is young.

Clean, I turned to the *Oyster Dunny*. I searched for signs of leaks and splashed water on the right rear tube to reveal the little bubbles of holes. I found a few below the waterline, and the valve on that side let out a steady hiss. I deflated the entire raft; it lay like a flayed gray whale on the beach. In midafternoon, when the sun was as vigorous as it was going to get, I took out my patching kit and went to work. I slapped a couple of small patches on, weighting them down with large, flat boulders. I also forced some glue into the gap between the valve and its rubber seat and held the two together for a half hour.

In early evening Max and I went on a slow walk around the drainage.

Max claimed to be a tracker. I followed behind him as he tracked wolf prints up from the beach, over and through the smooth, round river stones that separated the beach from the floodplain of the Dokdaon. He could point to a depression in the sand and explain what part of the pad it was and why it was different from anything else around it. Bear prints were easy to follow, and those of the wolf weren't hard, but there were other, smaller prints as well: some from sandpipers, some from smaller mammals, even from voles or mice, with their tails dragging between their tiny paw prints. We went along, hunched over like two bogus sleuths heading up the Dokdaon, and I realized again how little of the territory we owned. We had a beachhead about twenty-five yards long by fifty yards deep, which included our camp and a little of the floodplain. Every yard beyond that was a yard where we were visitors, watched instead of watching. The river was familiar; the shore was home; in the bush I was lost, a stranger, out of place and close to helpless.

As I walked behind Max I stopped, as though I'd heard something. I looked around, and I knew what it was I'd heard: a change. I no longer wanted to leave; I wanted to stay as long as I could, even though I knew I shouldn't be here. My life would return to its normal shape once I was in Maine; it would be impossible to ever bend it this direction again. I would go back to Maine eventually, but I was here now and that no longer seemed like a bad thing.

We walked along the creek until we came back to camp. I said to Max, "How about this . . ."

"The Sheslay?" said Max.

"Yeah. How did you know?" I asked. We hadn't talked about it.

"I knew that's what you wanted to do." He gave me a knowing smile.

"Yeah, I guess I do. How about you—is that okay with you?"

"Sure." He shrugged. "Sounds good." Apparently he didn't want to leave yet either.

I outlined the options as I saw them. If the kayak showed up, we'd go over to the Sheslay and out through Taku Inlet; if it didn't, we'd scoot down the Stikine. Max agreed.

Later Max said, "Bear."

I hopped up and went to where he was standing, pointing up the creek at a grove of cottonwood trees fifty yards away. "Where?" I asked.

"I saw him moving along the edge of those trees," Max said.

I didn't see anything. We ventured behind camp for a better look, but nothing was stirring. Still, Max decided it was time to pump a round into the chamber of the gun. He worked the pump on the barrel of the shotgun, and it stuck halfway down. "Oh shit," Max said. He jerked the pump back and forth, but it remained stuck, apparently forever.

———

Bears are charming. I know almost nothing about their psyches or about their habits or ethics. I just love the size of them, their strength and speed. I like their sharp teeth and huge claws, the thick fur, the way they amble, and what appears to be the intelligence in their beady eyes. I like it that I can anthropomorphize them—I like their independent and rugged character.

Before I began guiding, I thought of bears as harmless denizens of the woods. I could have gone on imagining them as circumspect—though large —creatures, wisely avoiding contact with humans, but I started to encounter them along rivers, in ways that made me see that while they were wary of humans, they weren't crippled by that wariness. Yet one of the rewards of a guiding life has been bear encounters, the times when I've come close to bears, with no harm on either side.

One night on the Rogue we had camped at a narrow beach, at the base of a steep bluff. In the middle of the night I was awakened by shouts. Another guide, a woman named Darrell, was yelling as though a romantic moment had gone sour. "Get out of here! Go away! Go!" I called out to Darrell, and she called back that there was a bear in camp and not to shine any lights. Soon she was banging on pots and pans, the classic bear repellent. "He's not leaving!" yelled Darrell, and my heart sank. As the lead guide on the trip, I was expected to do something about moments like this—moments when I would need my negligible wits.

"How's it going, Darrell?" I hollered a few moments later from inside my tent, where I lay warm next to my girlfriend.

"He won't leave. He just goes up the hill a few yards and comes back." I poked my head out of the tent and waited for my eyes to adjust. Then I saw the real reason Darrell hadn't wanted flashlights: she was standing naked in the middle of camp, banging on cookware.

Also naked, I slipped out of the tent and crouched near her, trying to keep a low profile. I heard the bear woof a time or two, and Darrell fiercely whispered, "That means he's mad."

"Let's give him something," I whispered back.

"No, that won't work; he'll want it all."

No problem, I thought.

We banged and clattered and yelled some more, and when we stopped we didn't hear any more bear. He didn't make any noise as he left, and even though I stayed awake the rest of the night waiting for him, he didn't come back.

That was the moment when my attitude about bears changed. I realized that my relationship to them was more complicated than I'd imagined and my understanding of them was limited. A few years later I was camped at White Pine, along the Middle Fork in Idaho. It is a slow stretch of river, with an open brushy flat across from camp. For no reason I woke in the middle of the night and sat up in my bag on the sand. There was a full moon, and as I gazed sleepily around, I caught some movement on the opposite shore. The movement became a smooth lumbering, a bear patrolling the driftwood and boulders of an old rock slide. It was a remarkable—even romantic—moment. We were the only ones awake, the bear and I, in the moonlight. The bright light reflected off his fur, and the grace of his movements was expressive, as affecting in its way as any symphony or opera or jazz riff or ballet.

In 1981 two other guides and I were flown over the Brooks Range to a gravel bar near the headwaters of the Noatak River. We had a few days to kill before the next trip, and we spent them organizing our gear and staying out of the rain that fell in torrents when it fell. One day I wandered up a ravine south of camp. Like many of the mountain tributaries of the Noatak, Angayu Creek cuts a narrow defile into the side of the canyon, an almost vertical channel. When I set out on my walk, I didn't follow the stream, since it was choked by alders—terrible country to wander in, when one is thinking of bears. Instead I went straight up the hill that formed the square corner of the confluence of the Noatak and the Angayu. From a little rock outcrop, I could look down upon the Noatak, upstream at Mt. Igikpak— the source of the Noatak and the highest peak in the Brooks Range—and up the steep canyon of the Angayu.

The Angayu went directly away from the Noatak for a half mile or so, then cut to the left in a ninety-degree angle. That turn was so sharp, I couldn't see anything around the corner, but the sun came down it like a spotlight, a bright, late-morning beam of light more rich than usual, making the elbow of the corner glow.

As I gazed about, keeping an eye out for bears—bears behind me, sneaking up from below, parachuting bears—I noticed another guide, Bruce Reitherman, climbing the ridge opposite me, that is, on the other side of the Angayu and around the corner, so that he was mostly on the Noatak side of the confluence. Turning back to the Angayu, I saw a squirming ball where the creek turned left. The ball was a grizzly. While grizzlies come in an assortment of colors, this one was so light as to be nearly blond. He sat on an outcropping of rock high above the stream, about two hundred yards from me, scratching himself. First he lay flat on his back and rocked his shoulders from side to side, scratching his spine; then he lifted his rear paw and batted himself on the ear, as a dog might. After this he sat flat on his bottom, like a baby propped up in front of a toy, and looked out over the canyon. It was as though he were both sunning himself and surveying his domain, playful and lordly. The sun coming down the canyon lit him in a reverential halo, making each hair in his fur spark. He was isolated in the canyon, suspended away from the canyon wall and above the river on his outcrop. His manner was so unself-conscious that he seemed to be utterly unaware of anything around him. I couldn't imagine a better, safer view of a grizzly.

After a few minutes he stirred, and began to descend from his perch toward the stream. It occurred to me that I ought to warn Bruce, if I could, that a bear was wandering in his neighborhood.

My rocky landing had a large flat boulder on it, about four feet high. The ground dropped directly away on either side of the boulder. I walked down toward the Noatak and spotted Bruce on the other side of the ravine. I waved my arms at him. That had no effect, so I shouted, although I wasn't happy about that, since I didn't want to make myself known to the bear in the ravine. After ten minutes of this, nothing had caught Bruce's attention, so I retreated to my boulder to see what my bear was up to.

As I walked back up to the rock, I had a curious sensation—the sudden knowledge that I was loose in the bush with a bear whose location I no longer knew. I had last seen him leaving his rock and heading down to the stream. I didn't know where he might have gone from there. He might even have headed my way. Still, I thought, I would have plenty of time to get back to my perch, spot him, and plan my measured withdrawal.

I labored up the last ten feet of the hill to the boulder. I reached the plateau and glanced at the rock. It had grown: it was six feet tall now, with a blondish lump. At the moment when I came to know—in that flashing, blinding, whizzing of brain circuitry that allows you to understand many things at once—that I had been stalked, that the bear had left his perch because he had smelled me and had walked directly to my spot, and that now there was a grizzly within hugging distance of me—the bear raised his huge head above the rock and looked at me. Our eyes locked, sentience on sentience.

The image and its attendant emotions will be with me always; they are so intense, I imagine they will survive me, just as sounds outlast the speaker and circulate forever in the universe, another addition to the cosmic stockpile of fear and terror. There wasn't the slightest pause, not a hint of one, before I turned and fled down the hill. This was a mistake: everything I'd ever told passengers about bears was that one must not show panic or try to run; you should withdraw slowly, facing the bear, letting the bear know that you consider it an equal and aren't prey for it.

Screw that. My response was so instant and unreflective, I might have been practicing for this moment my entire life. I turned, I ran. Straight downhill, nearly outrunning my feet. After fifty yards I ventured a glance over my shoulder to see if the bear was gaining. Nothing there, but I kept on, suspecting a trick. When I came to the level ground along the Noatak, I stopped, gasping, and looked all around. No bear. At the same moment I had turned and fled, the bear had probably done the same.

———

Max sat down to work on the gun, while I repacked our food in the river bags. The repacking was soothing, which was helpful when I saw Max fumbling with the gun. He dropped the shells into the sand as he unscrewed the barrel, then dropped the screwdriver he was using, then his bandana, then the spring for the loading chamber. I carefully placed the dried apricots into a river bag marked "lunch." The river streamed past, swirling, dipping, boiling, smooth.

8 *Portage*

Sid hesitated only long enough to bite a chunk off a panatella cigar to renew
his chaw, then he called out to the native boy deckhand who was lolling
on the scow that the bow of our boat pushed ahead of us, "Willie, get the
sounder working, I'm going to take her through that hole in the woods."
— "The Dean of Alaskan Rivermen"

I lay in my bag, one thought repeating itself: "I miss my wife." I'd written it the night before; it sat there so nakedly on the page that it appeared to mean I was prostrate with grief, overcome to the point where that was all I could write. Actually, it meant just that: I missed her, her voice, her face, her presence. And it led to other thoughts: Did she make it home okay with the kids? Is she well? How is the baby?

When I'd last seen her she'd been crying, afraid to get into a car because her huge stomach made her feel claustrophobic and because her cracked tailbone made it painful to sit. I'd left anyway. The memory of leaving made my heart race and sweat break out on my brow — the honest weight of guilt on my chest.

I was a puzzle to myself, that I was beside the Dokdaon given all of that. Some days I tortured myself by imagining the guilt I would feel if something went wrong. I couldn't do it. I could picture Sid, looking grim and tight lipped, but going on. He was forty-five when his son died, and probably he and Hazel thought they were too old to try again. This, for him, I could imagine: that at forty-five the future doesn't stretch out so far, and he knows that there isn't time to try again, to have another child. In the tent I tried very hard to think about other things.

It drizzled most of the night, and the clouds in the morning were low—big, puffy clouds, as though we were at the center of a storm. I had the feeling we wouldn't be seeing the plane from Telegraph Creek for a while. But the first unusual sound of the morning—other than the river, the creek, the wind in the trees, birds resting, then flying on—was of a plane coming from upstream. A blue-and-white Cessna. The pilot flew over us once, then went downriver, came around again through the canyon—which, with the plane filling it up, became a tiny place—then circled back once more. It looked as though he were going to disappear downriver, but he looped back one more time and dropped the plane onto the river not far below our beach, then taxied upstream to us with a roar. He slid into the sand, let the engine die, popped open his door, and stepped out onto a pontoon.

Some bush pilots buy into their image all the way, with fancy cowboy boots and belt buckles and drug-agent sunglasses; others eschew all trappings, unaware of the clothes they wear or the way they appear or even that they have an appearance. Ron Jansen was a member of that latter group. He was a little over six feet tall, with a dirty beard, a scar on his nose, a greasy baseball cap, a shirt that was a hand-me-down from someone's teenage cousin, and a weird pair of polyester gray pants, which were ill-fitting and hung low on his hips, creating the impression that he was misshapen in some way. He wore a pair of high-top, rubber-rimmed sneakers that had once been white. He looked to be about fifty.

He stepped off the pontoon and onto the beach, saying, "Didn't think I'd make it in here, goddamn it."

We introduced ourselves and helped him tie up the plane; then we listened to him tell about the rough landing. I apologized for needing him to fly in here, but Ron shrugged it off. "Oh hell, I always wanted to see if I could land here anyhow. It's a tight fucking spot, though; there isn't a lot of room to fuck-up in here."

We walked around the gravel bar and showed Ron a weird tripod and bear skeleton we'd found up the drainage a ways. "Fucking poachers," he announced and scuffed at the skeleton with his tennis shoe. We asked Ron for news of the world; he didn't know of any, he said, since he hadn't paid attention for years. Besides, "my memory's not too good anyhow—first you forget names, then faces, and then to zip up, and then to zip down."

"Any sign of our kayak?" I ventured.

Ron shook his head. "Not a fucking thing," he said. "Never showed up and I never heard a fucking thing about it. The airline called, but that's all they said: 'no fucking kayak.'"

Max and I looked at each other. It was settled. The plan had been, no kayak, no Sheslay. We were headed back down the Stikine, a repeat, for me, of 1988. The raft, all our gear, would have to be set up again for a float downstream.

We walked back to the beach. Already I was having pangs of regret, anticipatory regret, regret at the regret I was going to have if we settled for the Stikine again. I couldn't stand it.

"Do you have a few minutes, Ron, while we figure this out?" I asked.

"Oh fuck, sure," he said. "I've got nowhere to be today." Max and I walked beside the eddy while we talked it over. Everything argued for us leaving as quickly as we could, via the Stikine. There are times, though, when the siren calls of Experience are too strong to resist. If I continued to ignore my obligations, I could see new waters, new places, maybe have a thrill or two. As usual I was torn between what I should do and what I was tempted to do. But I was here; Pat had said she understood why I needed to go; if there were any problems at home, surely Ron would have brought that message in. Thus I reasoned with myself.

I asked Ron what it would cost to fly us out to Telegraph Creek, then to the Hackett-Sheslay area, and he squinted while he calculated. It would be about $400 Canadian, he announced, with "just enough left over for a jug."

That was too much for me; I wondered aloud if the airline would cover it. Ron thought they probably would, and since he was headed back to Telegraph Creek, he was willing to call them on the radiophone and find out.

I looked at Max. "Is that all right?" Max grinned that foolish grin of his, so I knew it was.

We arranged with Ron that he would come back within three hours if the answer was yes, and cart us away; if the answer was no or he couldn't get an answer, then he wouldn't return at all, and after three hours we would draw our own conclusions and float on.

Ron pushed off and crawled into the cockpit. He spun the plane upstream and motored as high up our eddy as he could. He edged into the current, let the current turn the plane, and gunned the engine. Soon he was up on step, bouncing along the top of the chop in the river, then bounding into the air. His ascent was sluggish at first, but he swept to the south and then to the east toward Telegraph Creek, and the upstream wind caught him and he shot past us.

At least for the next few hours we were stuck. It was about one; we wouldn't see him before three at the earliest. We went back to relaxing, stretching out on the beach, Max fooling with the stupid gun again.

Time ticked slowly. At three o'clock I stirred. There was only an hour left until our deadline, and we knew we didn't want to spend another night here by the Dokdaon; if Ron didn't show, we would float. I began setting up our gear again. We stumbled around, moving slowly so that, should Ron appear, we wouldn't be forced to strip it all back down.

At 3:30 we rolled out the raft.

At 3:45 we pumped, slowly, in a mime show of effort.

By 3:55 I had given up. Despite my earlier ambivalence, I was now devoted to the idea of the Sheslay; the thought of repeating the Stikine was appalling.

"This sucks," said Max.

"Gahhh," I groaned, trying not to talk or think.

I achieved the zenlike condition of complete and total surrender to the truth that Ron wasn't coming back; the raft was pumped up; some of the rigging was done. I stopped, then Max stopped. "What's that?" he asked.

"A plane," I said, even though I didn't know.

The sound was too far off and tinny to recognize. It could be a plane or a boat or even just our ears, ringing in anticipation. Then suddenly above our heads, appearing over the edge of the bluff across the river, the plane, Ron's plane, exploded into view, blue and white. The theme from *Rocky* played in the background.

"All right!" I shouted, and Max whipped his hat off to wave. "Saved!" he yelled.

Ron passed over us several times, then dropped the plane down on the river. He landed just as he had the first time, taxied as he had before. Then he spun the plane in a half circle and flew away.

It was like some cruel joke, taken to absurd extremes, as though Ron would fly all the way in here just to tease us. Max and I looked at each other—if my face looked like Max's, then I had a crushed expression. The Cessna banked steeply to the left and headed back toward Telegraph Creek. "What the fuck?" Max complained.

The blue and white was lost in the cottonwoods that blocked our view. "What happened? I don't get this," I moaned, still not believing he had left. It didn't make sense, but the evidence was clear: the plane was leaving. Indeed, it seemed to have vanished.

We could still hear it, though, a thin buzzing long after it should have faded; the buzzing grew louder again, and once more the plane appeared over the bluff across the river, and once more it swooped up and down the canyon a few times, then came fluttering toward us, the pontoons lowering gently onto the river, the propeller slowing. Then Ron taxied roaring into the beach.

Beached, Ron popped out of the plane. "What the fuck's going on, guys?" he said.

"What was that all about?" Max asked.

"Fucking current was too strong the first time," he said, stepping onto our beach. "It just about knocked me over, so I figured I'd better get the fuck out of there."

"What's the word, Ron?" I interrupted. "Are they going to pay?"

"Hell yes," he said with a vigorous nod of his head.

"They'll shuttle us over to the Sheslay?" I pressed.

"Well, that's the message I got," he said. "Say, how much does this shit weigh?" he added, kicking our gear.

"Not too much," I said, avoiding that topic. Max and I deflated and rolled the raft as fast as we could. Another unearned experience was about to be upon us, and we were quick to take advantage of it.

Ron looked our gear over and pointed at various pieces, and we did the lugging. I told Ron that the equipment and Max and I weighed no more than seven hundred pounds, which was an exaggeration but not quite a lie, I thought. We managed to get it all in, leaving a tiny square for Max to sit in on the second seat. I sat in front with an ammo box on my lap, reminding me of a time I had left a village in the Brooks Range in a plane so full that I'd had to either hold a big can of beans on my lap or leave it behind. For some reason I held on to it.

As we lifted off the river and banked over Dokdaon Creek, I spotted a set of tracks coming down the creek, crossing it, and heading up the Stikine behind where we had been. From the air I couldn't tell whose they were—moose, bear, or wolf—but they looked clear enough to have been made during the last couple of days. A reminder once again of how little of the country we controlled and how little we knew about what was going on around us.

We craned to look back up the Chutine to the familiar mountains around Dirst Creek, and we searched out the plateaus to the east and south, where the headwaters of the Stikine were. The clouds were an endless series of flatbottoms, marching toward all horizons. It was a strange sensation, to be lifted from our riparian life into this mechanical one, and even more strange to be returning to Telegraph Creek, a place which, once you've left, you assume you will never see again.

⸺

Hazel B. No. 3 was built in Wrangell in 1917. The *Hazel B. No. 4* appeared in 1919. The second *Hazel B. No. 2* was also built in Wrangell, in 1925. The third *Hazel B. No. 2*, the biggest boat Sid ever owned (a hundred feet long, with twin 135-horsepower engines), was launched in Seattle in 1932. The second *Hazel B. No. 1* came out in 1941.

During World War II, Sid and Hill ran freight for the army on the Stikine. In 1952 Harry, Sid's elder brother, died at eighty-three. In 1954 Hazel was gone, following "an illness of several weeks," the obituary said. In early June Sid took her body south to Seattle from Wrangell, where they had been opening up the river for the year. It was the second time he'd had to accompany a body south to Oak Harbor, the first being fifty-six years before with his brother Ed. That would have been a grim journey, compounded by the memory of the earlier trip and of how a lifetime had passed since then.

By the eleventh of June, Sid had returned to the river. Bob DeArmond, a Juneau journalist and historian, took a trip with Sid later that summer and remembered that he was subdued. " 'I have just lost my mate' Sid said several times," DeArmond recalled.

Sid's last trip upriver was in that year. I wish I knew what that final trip was like for him, and whether he knew it was the last one, and if so, how he felt about that: the end to a lifetime of rivers. By 1955 he was living in a nursing home in Oak Harbor, and on June 28 of 1963, he died. Nobody tells any stories about those last years.

—

We landed on a pond near Ron's house. After we taxied up to his dock and unloaded, Ron suggested suspiciously that we weigh our gear on his old cast-iron scale. I was embarrassed to see that the total was 972 pounds, which was about 170 pounds over the maximum payload for the plane. Ron turned pale, looked a little disgusted, and for a while wasn't very cheerful.

He offered to let us stay on his property, though, since we wouldn't be able to fly out until morning. It was late afternoon by then, and Ron wheeled us into town in his truck. I hoped something had changed in the three years since I'd been there last, that there would be a newly discovered *Hazel B.*, a Sid Barrington Museum, an annual Barrington parade, something.

No luck. Telegraph Creek was just the same. Being there was like stepping out of one time and into another. We had been on our own for nine days, with only each other for company and moving to our own whims and rhythms. Being in town, even a town like Telegraph Creek, is a far different thing than being in the bush.

The Riversong Café was still there, the hub of the town, and there still weren't many tourists. I heard about a company that sometimes ran kayaking trips down the Stikine, and hunters used Telegraph Creek as the jump-off for trips into lodges hidden back in the hills. Government scientists seemed to be the most frequent visitors, along with the occasional adventuresome traveler who might wander in from Dease Lake on the dirt spur.

We stopped into the café for coffee and rolls—fresh cinnamon ones. There were a few kids; otherwise it was all men inside when we arrived. We took our coffee cups to sit at a table and stayed for an hour, chatting with the locals, telling our stories. Two government geologists who were working in the hills came in, and we told them about Chutine Lake. They snapped to attention when we mentioned the lake, and they were envious, like explorers hearing of a hidden temple. When we mentioned the red knob of rock we had seen, they became intense—"It was red?" they asked. "Bright red or dull red?"

"Bright, and it was all red, not a mix of other colors," Max explained.

The geologists looked at each other. "We've got to find a way to get in there," one said to the other.

Later we returned to Ron's place. Ron was hosting another geologist, a graduate student, for the summer. The student told terrible stories about being chased in the hills by old grizzlies, ones whose teeth had worn down over the years, whose nerves were so exposed that it sent the bears into a killing madness, he said. He compensated for these grim tales by giving us four slugs for our gun, which seemed pitiful when compared to these misanthropic bears.

Max borrowed some of Ron's tools and stripped the gun, greased it, and repaired it as best he could. Ron was working on a platform to use in rolling gasoline drums into his plane, and I remembered Dan Baldwin's crushed foot in Wrangell. I helped Ron hammer a few nails for the ramp in his shed, which had a twisted, ruined skeleton of a plane along one wall. I walked past it a few times before it registered that this was probably one of Ron's planes. "Hey," I called. "What's the story with this one?" And I pointed at the corpse.

"Smashed it at the pond," he said without taking his eyes off the ramp.

I stared at the cruelly twisted hunk of metal, then at Ron; I tried to imagine the latter inside the former. I couldn't do it.

He'd been attempting to land with a tailwind, he explained, but hadn't been able to stop at the end of the pond and had kept going. "I just kept on flying it until it stopped moving," he said, straightening up and stretching his back.

"Jeez," I said, "that must have been something."

"Yeah," he said, hammering again. "The fucking trees were snapping all around me. The wings tore off and the fucking engine was just about in my lap when I stopped, and there wasn't a scratch on me. I jumped right out of the fucking plane and walked on home. It was something, alright," he added.

We slept on the floor of Ron's freshly painted bunkhouse, with the door open to keep the paint fumes from killing us. About four, when it was already light, I was besieged by mosquitoes, which got so thick that I twisted my rain fly around my head to keep them off. Between the fumes and the mosquitoes, I was ready to get back to the bush.

At six Ron came to get us. We drank a quick cup of coffee, ate two pieces of toast, and drove out to the town strip. We loaded Ron's second plane, a 185 on wheels, this time with me in back, trapped among the gear. There were flat-bottomed puffy clouds hovering over all of interior British Columbia. All of the land I could see, while drier and a bit less steep than classic mountain terrain—than the Sawtooths in Idaho, say—was wild enough, filled with enough secret spots and valleys, to make me wish I was there, everywhere, at every place my eye touched, all at the same moment.

BOOK III *Sheslay*

The River. That is what they talk about. To love the river is to be obsessed, and the river people have given themselves over willingly to that obsession. . . . They like to get together and talk about things which are a terrific bore to everyone but their fellow-obsessives. Flips, user-days, holes, sucking eddies, nylon track shorts, death. Famous River Disasters.

—Rene Dowling, "Boatmen"

9　Running Blind

Visions! omens! hallucinations! miracles! ecstasies! gone down
the American river!

Breakthroughs! over the river! flips and crucifixions!

Real holy laughter in the river!
  —Allen Ginsberg, "Howl"

Canadian maps show a dot marked "Sheslay" as though a village exists,
but it doesn't. There is just a dirt strip that a mining company owns, and
the only people around when we landed were part of the mining crew. We
jounced down the runway, and some of the crew came down to see who
we were. They knew Ron and weren't much interested in us, so they went
back up to their shack with Ron while Max and I accepted help from a
young Tahltan named Dale. He gave us a ride down to the tiny waterway
of Egnell Creek in his ATV and trailer, and he dropped us near an abandoned orchard next to a crumbling cabin—the real Sheslay, I suppose. He
didn't stick around to chat but unloaded us, accepted a few bucks, and was
off. From there we still had a quarter-mile walk to a place where we could
launch the *Oyster Dunny*.

We were left in brushy bottomland, in a valley created by the confluence
of several rivers and the ending of some minor ranges. The bugs were thick,
and the dense brush was gloomy and stifling and hot. Battling the night of
bad sleep, we had a silent march, schlepping the gear the quarter mile down
into the swampy, wet swale. Abused by mosquitoes, we trudged back and

forth into this heart-of-darkness place along the tiny creek. I had a brief vision, a memory of putting-in on the Rio Atoyac in Mexico, where we walked down into the canyon on a thin, steep trail, carrying a raft rolled around an oar on our shoulders, like a trussed-up pig, and met a wizened old woodcutter coming up from the river with a donkey loaded with wood. We passed each other in a booming clash of cultures, colors, and ambitions.

When finally we had the gear piled by the creek, Max and I pumped up the *Oyster Dunny*, rigged the cargo net in back, and tied on the safety line. "Coffee," I said.

"Oh, man, let's go," Max groaned, slapping a mosquito into oblivion. "Let's get out of here."

"Coffee," I repeated, pulling open one of the food bags.

We sat on the edge of the raft while we waited for the water to boil. Slumped, we nibbled on crackers. My head still rang from breathing paint fumes all night.

When the water was ready, I made a cup of instant coffee; Max urged me to drink it instantly. He wanted to make time, move along. He had called his girlfriend, Katrina, on a radiophone from Telegraph Creek, and that had convinced him that things were going to work out, and made him anxious again to get downriver. I had called home, too, but hadn't been able to make a connection. Still, I wanted to sit and meditate on this latest chapter of setting off. Creekside wasn't a pleasant place to be, and buried deep within the bush we couldn't see anything of the more impressive surroundings, but the journey of a thousand miles begins beneath one's feet, said Lao Tzu, so I stared at my feet a little longer.

Finally we dragged the *Oyster Dunny* into the creek, which was so small, it was dwarfed by the raft. It was barely a creek—more of a freshet—and it was choked with scrub brush and bushes and deadfalls. We pulled ourselves along using the branches arching overhead until the creek joined the Hackett, a slightly larger, faster version of the Egnell. The Hackett was choked with debris at every turn, too, and ran faster. We had to stop at the beginning of each turn, jump out while holding tight to the raft and slide it around the corner into a tangle of branches, then hop onto the pile to pull the raft over it. If the jams had been bigger and the current stronger, we might have been in trouble. But we were able to drag the raft over or kick our way through the jams to clear a path for it. There was no such thing as a straight section to the Hackett. It was all twists and corners, a small stream trying to find its way out of the brush.

The brush at last ended, giving way to a wide basin and a broad, fast, open river. The Hackett ended, too, and became the Sheslay, the two coming into each other from nearly opposite directions. The Sheslay, where it exited from the same mountains that had housed the Barrington and the Chutine, was a washboard river, a steady white flush between steep ridges. Once again I was reminded of the flaws in my planning: we couldn't possibly have made it down the Sheslay from the headwaters north of Chutine Lake. The river was a flume of water, only inches deep, and we wouldn't have been able to sink a paddle into it to guide the raft. Utterly helpless, we would have bounced like a crazed cork down the river. Still, the terrain it came from looked bold. Our side of the confluence was shallow and insipid; the Sheslay side was Byronic, as it poured down from the heights.

At a big pool at the confluence, we stopped to fish. A moose horn buried in the mud caught Max's eye. "Hey, mind if we take this along?" he said.

"What for?" I asked. "What are you going to do with it?"

"I don't know. It'll be a good-luck charm or something. Maybe I'll put it in my garden and watch it disintegrate." We tied the moose horn on the bow of the raft through the front D-ring and entered the fast Sheslay.

The Sheslay swept around one gravelled corner, then another. The first turns we took tentatively, hugging the inside shore just in case we had to stop to scout. After a few corners, though, we could see how things were going and could feel the character of the river, and we quit worrying and enjoyed the ride.

Once again I was thrilled by the thrill of new water—there is nothing like it. When you don't know what is around the first corner or where any other turn is after that, when every landscape and every perspective is entirely new. How many things in an adult's world are new and rare?

The river charged on in the first miles—similar to the speed at the beginning of the Chutine, except the valley was wider here, with completely different vegetation: fewer evergreens, fewer bushes on shore, fewer anything, even though we were only a few dozen miles from the Chutine. The Sheslay had cut a wide valley, topped by a short bluff, past which we could only rarely see. The bluff was layered in bands of bright colors, the bands bending and dipping toward the river.

After about five miles, the river slowed, as the precipitous drop from the confluence eased, and the river took on the character of an aimless meander through a level valley. A high ceiling of grayness covered the valley; beneath that moved individual squalls. We could see them slide downstream at us, sometimes missing, sometimes dusting us, while others snuck over a rim of the valley and found us. We drifted along, alternately taking off and putting on rain gear as the squalls approached and retreated. We slid to the western edge of the valley, then to the east, then back again.

The Stikine would have been lovely and impressive and grand, but this was new, a mystery, whose climax was somewhere downstream. I was entirely satisfied, if sleepy, as we floated beneath new skies. As long as I didn't think about my wife or baby.

The river slowed as we continued, as though it were emptying into a lake or building up to a waterfall. I didn't expect either to happen, but something seemed to be in the offing. Before leaving California I'd found a doctor in Juneau—known as Dr. Vacation because he spent so much time in the bush—who had run the Sheslay a few years before, in late summer. Over the phone he had described it as a beautiful river, with lots of animals, in an ignored canyon. I asked him about rapids. He said there were two: "a pretty good one midway through the canyon, and then the big one at the end."

We stopped after a few hours for lunch. We fell asleep on the *Dunny* and woke in the rain, which instantly became sunshine. We were blessed by not having any wind, and in midafternoon the clouds lifted and dissolved. The canyon was weirdly quiet. Quiet, because there was no wind; quiet, because the current was slow and steady; quiet, because it was quieter than Telegraph Creek, that roaring town. One of the few sounds was that of hummingbirds dive-bombing us because of the red rain jackets we wore.

We looked for a large drainage coming in from the left, which according to my map would be the Samotua River. But we kept passing drainages of one sort or another that we thought might have been it, until late in the afternoon, after many hours on the river, when we saw a very large river descending upon us from the left. It could have been one of two tributaries; I pronounced it the Samotua.

We pulled in on the upstream side of the confluence, where the river had left a swath of gravel a quarter mile long, which tilted from the upstream side down across the tributary to a lower patch. The gravel was broken by ridges, which held pockets of standing water. It was like a river canyon in miniature, complete with braids, islands, and ponds.

We noticed a moose standing on the lower gravel bar watching us. The only inviting camping spots were on the moose's side of the tributary, yet intruding upon her space simply so we could have a nice bed seemed rude. We searched for a spot, while the moose stood her ground, defiant in the face of the enormous threat we posed, but there wasn't any place that would do. The moose would have to go.

We drifted a few yards to the lower bar. When we started unloading, the moose finally turned around and trotted off, in that weird moose gait, something huge and ungainly trying to maintain its dignity, holding its head aloft, unruffled, while its lower parts scuttle and wobble.

The sky emptied as we worked. The first half of the day had made me fear we had turned the corner into bad weather. But now it looked as though we were going to get lucky again. Downstream on our side was a mountain, unnamed on our map, which looked a bit like Mt. Katahdin in Maine: both have flat tops which stretch horizontally and have relatively regular flanks descending from those tops. The more I looked at that mountain and what seemed to be a matching one across the river, the more something boiled in my brain, made a little noise, a chord in a minor key. No specific thought came to the surface, but something was stirring.

After dinner I was refreshed enough to go and get my Jew's harp from the raft. The only instruments I took on rivers when I was a guide were a Jew's harp and, in the first few years, a flute. The flute, which I played poorly, was an old, unvaluable thing that used to belong to one of my sisters. I got good enough on the flute to improvise a little, and I could also make up my own vaguely Irish-sounding melodies. Back then I hoped this would be a great seducer on the river.

The flute came to an ignoble end early in my guiding career. Like Sid I had a few accidents in my first years; the worst was on the Tuolumne, at a place called Chicken Shot. I didn't make it through a narrow slot through three large boulders, and I wedged my raft on a log which itself was wedged among the boulders.

My passengers floated away, as did my baggage, while I struggled with the raft for an hour, trying to free it but horrified at the idea of being in the water with it. The raft vibrated like some palsied thing. This was an epiphanetic moment, when I came to see water in a new way.

Finally I gave up; it was sunset, and dinner had to be cooked and gear needed to be dried and, in some cases, found. When I finally left the raft, slipping into the water and floating down to camp in my life jacket, the waters had become darkly smooth. It was one of the more depressing swims of my life.

The beach below Chicken Shot looked like a refugee camp. Gear was spread out over the rocks, and people were huddled around the fire in their wet clothes. Most of the baggage belonging to the passengers had made it into camp, even though soaked, but the guides were big losers: Brent had lost everything, including three hundred dollars in cash; Gloystein was now missing a sleeping bag and some of his clothes. I had my bag and a few clothes, but my favorite pair of sneakers—white hightops with little yellow smiley faces all over them—were gone. And so was the flute.

We divided gear as best we could, so everyone had something to sleep in, and we made it through the night, although no one—not the passengers, not the guides—spoke to me. By morning the water had dropped and the raft was easy to free, and the disaster seemed more like an adventure, but the flute was still gone.

A week later I was rigging a boat at Camp Nine, the put-in for the Stanislaus, when a guide from another company came up. He was, like most guides, another stringy, pot-smoking hipster.

"Hey, man," he said, "are you the guy that lost the flute on the T.?"

My fame had spread rapidly: the story of the guide whose raft had spent the night at Chicken Shot and whose flute had sunk to the bottom of the Tuolumne. This is the sort of thing that can make a lasting reputation in whitewater circles. "Yeah, that's me," I admitted. "Sank the fucker near Driftwood."

"Well, someone found it," he told me.

"You're kidding." I'd assumed it was gone forever; I almost hoped it was, so the story would die.

"Nope, a guy from OARS saw it a few days ago just downstream from the Shot when he went to get water. It was sitting there a few feet off shore."

A couple of days later, I retrieved the flute, but it was worthless. So the only instrument I took on trips afterwards was the Jew's harp, which I plucked now out of my ammo box. I headed back to camp with it and got within a few yards of the tent when something made me lift my head. There was no movement, and the gray blended in well with the willows and aspens—I looked and there was the wolf.

In eighteen years of guiding in wild places, the one large predator I hadn't seen was a wolf. It was the mystery animal, the one everyone wants to encounter but knows they probably won't; the one that is too rare, too smart to be seen.

The mythical creature stood about thirty yards away, in the gravel between where the aspens ended and the Samotua began. The wolf patiently turned its head from side to side, keeping an eye on me all the while.

"Max," I called, sotto voce. "Wolf!"

My voce hadn't carried far enough. "What?" he asked, looking up from his kneeling position to see where I was, not where the wolf was.

"Wolf!" I said again, more intently.

Now it registered. "Where?!" he said, spinning around.

"There." I pointed.

Max crouched, as though to present a lower profile. Then he and I froze, watching the wolf watching us.

The wolf was larger than I expected, and it had that apparently unshakeable calm one expects from a wolf—it seemed master of the situation, aware of everything and in control of it all, perfectly measured in its movements. The wolf kept swiveling its head; I thought it might be scanning the landscape, as though passing through this place was crucial to it. When it tossed its head to one side, it seemed to be looking at something behind.

"Pretty cool, huh?" I said to Max.

Max whispered, "The best."

"Ever seen one before?" I asked.

Max shook his head. "Never. Always wanted to."

The wolf dropped its big head and took a few paces closer, then looked up and around and turned so quickly, we hardly realized it had moved.

"He's gone," Max said, disappointed.

We stayed as we were, watching for a return, but nothing did. The wolf was thoroughly gone.

"Let's go check out the prints," I suggested.

We hadn't performed our usual exploring of the terrain when we pulled into camp, and we were appalled to find a huge grizzly print near our tent. I've never gotten used to the size of grizzly prints; they always seem monstrous. This one was honestly huge, truly huge, thoroughly huge, completely huge. I set a knife next to it, and the print dwarfed the knife. I put my hand beside it, and my hand looked like a child's. I placed my gum boot down, and finally the print looked like something with ordinary proportions. I measured it at eleven and a half inches. The print's edges were as sharp as a shadow's; the Samotua had receded in the previous day or two, and the bear had walked here after the water's drop.

The wolf tracks were of a ghost, it seemed. Something had been here, and now these were all that was left. The tracks were tangible, but they were the idea, not the thing itself. We got a surprise when we walked a few feet up the creek: little tracks, little wolf tracks, showing that our wolf had been a mother traveling with two pups. Farther along we saw that the two small sets alongside the larger print had made their way down the Samotua; then the two little ones ended, and the larger one kept coming to the place where she'd seen us.

Ours was a ragged trip, filled with stops and starts, with ambivalence and defeats. We'd had to hire a way into the place and had relied on others to move us around, but still—we were here, and for the first time I'd seen a wolf in the wild. Not just my first wolf but a mother with pups. I felt honored, rich, lucky.

We wandered back to camp, following one set of prints or another. Within our narrow gravel strip, we could see wolf, grizzly, and moose tracks, plus the slither trail a beaver makes with its tail. A plethora of wildlife. I stopped to horrify myself once more at the bear print.

The evening glowed: because of the wolf, the river, the improving sky. It had cleared, with a few pink-and-black clouds lit up by the setting sun. The color of those clouds—pink on the edges, black in the middle—was exactly like the classic description of a melanoma, I thought. The sun tried to set behind the Katahdin-like hill downstream but couldn't. It dipped below one part of the hill, then came up again on the other side, then sank into the canyon.

I began playing the harp. It is a great wilderness instrument: small and light and weird. Most novice harpers let the striker hit them in the teeth, which not only hurts but also spoils the notes. There isn't much you can do with melody; it's mostly a rhythm instrument, although one can create some interesting sounds by opening or closing the throat and by breathing forcefully in or out.

Sitting down by the river, I followed my own song, going where it wanted to go. In this miniature jam, I walked with the tune back and forth on the beach. Playing was good, but the river and the canyon transformed it into more. Rivers are soul fertilizer, enriching us while they pass by. It is to the riverside I go to drink a cup of coffee in the morning or a beer at night, to think, or to find pleasure: while I have a hard time reading if I am too close to the river's edge—a clash of pleasures—I can sit next to a river for hours or play the harp, especially beside a river like the Sheslay.

It was an unmarred night—not a trace of clouds or wind—and while I prepared for sleep, I saw a black bear appear quietly out of the brush at the lower end of the bar, walk downstream a ways, toward where the moose had been earlier, and disappear into the brush. It was a sign of how good it felt to be back in the bush that the appearance of the bear hardly seemed unusual. I slept the sleep of the angels that night, untroubled by anything.

I finished a daydream about riding with Sid down the Stikine and stretched—nothing but blue through the netting at the top of the tent. It was like being reborn: into a fresh, clean world, one that sparkled with energy and vigor. I unzipped the front door and stuck my head through to find a perfect world outside. Cool, sweet air and a river ever flowing, ever onward. I scrambled out of the bag. I couldn't wait to encounter the new day and the downstream adventures.

After breakfast, and another visit to both the bear and wolf prints—so big, so cute—I looked over our map again. Max had lost interest in my map gymnastics. We could always be where I thought we were, or somewhere else, and there was no way of telling for sure. He let me work on the maps, while he messed around with the fishing pole and seemed lost in his thoughts of Katrina and his new life.

No matter where I thought we were on the maps, a couple of things were clear about the place where we actually stood: the canyon was tightening up downstream, the Sheslay was now one channel, and the current had picked up. Until this morning I had thought the speed was a result of the tributary entering; now I saw that the river simply dropped downstream, not dramatically, but far more steeply than it had in yesterday's stretch. On this blessed day I thought that would be fun.

We dragged the *Dunny* off the mud flats and were immediately swept downstream, at a pace far faster than anything since the start of the Chutine. The river pitched to the left and out of sight around a slight right-hand turn. We could feel ourselves dropping down, into something rather than on the top of it. The canyon closed in and now stood above us, near us, dotted by trees. The trees were thin, but they marched up the hills in ragged ranks.

We stopped for lunch at another large tributary from the left, which could only be the Tatsatua. Unlike the Samotua, this was a single, swift ribbon that left only a narrow wedge of flat land at the confluence as a place to sit. We ate lunch there and admired the Tatsatua's clean, pellucid water.

On the map the contour lines were pressing closer to the river and closer to each other in the section ahead. This meant the river channel would have less room to expand, which meant it inevitably would have rapids. A constricted channel sooner or later has to drop, and when it did we would drop with it.

"This is cool," I said to Max. "Running a new river is like being young all over again."

"You were young once?" Max asked. He was grinning, sharp dimples etched in his cheeks.

"I think so. I barely remember. Man, I'm loving this."

"I am, too," Max said, happily. "This river stuff is alright."

As on the day before, every moment, every part of the river and canyon, was fresh. The wind off the water was unlike any other wind, the perspective on every foot of terrain an original one. The freshness of it would strike even the most experienced river guide, until he found himself slipping into thinking that this corner looked like the last one, this cliff reminded him of one in Idaho, or Alaska, or those ripples of any ripple from Maine to Mexico.

The river dropped, the canyon tightened more, and before too long we came to a rapid—a legitimate, frothing rapid. I looked at Max, Max looked at me. "Is this it?" Max asked, referring to the first drop Dr. Vacation had described.

We pulled over on the right bank, where a tumbling little creek spilled out of the rocks. I searched for signs of the tight walls that Dr. Vacation had said would be a marker. I couldn't see them or much of anything, as the trees and brush blocked views. "This can't be it," I told Max several times.

"How do you know?" he asked, but he was only referring to my map-reading failings, not disagreeing.

We walked downstream over the bread-loaf-sized stones until we had a clear view of the rapid. It was a series of standing waves, two or three feet high, created by a drop in elevation and by a wall on the left jutting in a few feet, the only obstacle in the rapid. The current pushed from the center down to the left, where it slapped into the wall. We searched past the rapid for its run-out. It seemed smooth, as far as I could see. There might be a braid downstream going around a small island, but the way looked clear—as far as I could see.

We went back to the raft, and I explained what I wanted. It was the first instruction I'd given Max since we hit the Stikine. We had become practiced at light paddling, at working together, sort of. This would be different; I would actually have to give commands. "We'll run the center of the waves," I said, pointing downstream. Max squinted. "Be prepared to paddle away from the wall if it looks as though the current is going to push us there; then we'll take a quick peek once we pass the wall to see what's downstream."

"Yeah, good, let's go," Max said, jazzed. It was fine to have some adrenaline. We looked over the gear, tightened it a little, and Max got in. As always, he took the right. I untied the *Dunny*, coiled the rope and fixed it to the bow, then pushed off and jumped into my spot on the left. The raft moved sluggishly out of the eddy. Then the current grabbed us and we were paddling straight into the first small wave.

We slid into the wave and began to bounce as we hit the bigger ones. We lifted and dropped, plunged and reared, and I shouted to let Max know that this was okay, this was fun and good. I reached forward with my paddle to twist us a little to the right, so that we slid past the wall.

Max was grinning wildly when we reached the bottom.

"That was nice," I gushed, just as something was dawning on me. Not consciously, not rationally, barely an instinct; eighteen years of river running responding to the message the topography had been sending. I stood up and looked downstream.

10   *Pool and Drop*

What you do, see, is you tuck your butt right up against the big rock,
like this, see, and slide off but hold your angle and pull right to avoid the
thumblike rock downstream, which you could wrap on bigger than shit.
When the flow's down to two feet, there's a small fuck-you rock in the
channel just above the thumb.
—river guide, Middle Fork of the Salmon

The river was forcing us onto a ten-foot-tall logjam. The channel to
the right in front of the jam wouldn't let us through; the left channel was
blocked from view—I couldn't tell whether it would go or not. My sudden
standing had alarmed Max, and he jerked his head around and said, "This
looks interesting," again.

"Fuck," I said, scanning the river. We had to do something, and now. I
dropped onto the tube and back-paddled furiously.

Max joined in with as much energy as I'd ever seen him do anything,
while I waited for the left channel to reveal itself. Then suddenly we had
no choice: we couldn't get back to the right even if we'd wanted to. If the
left channel was blocked . . .

We edged past the jam and into the left channel, and I saw that there
were two more channels beyond, each spilling hard to the right, back to
join the main channel. They were formed by more logjams, and we couldn't
get past either of them. We had to make this first drop to the right. I yelled,
"Go! Dig!" and we shot ahead, both of us rocking forward with the effort,
into the slot and down.

We were clear then, back in the main channel. "Shit," I said, shaking my head, looking downstream at what seemed to be an entirely different river.

Max chuckled. "That was something, huh? What happened?"

"Too much water. Too much current," I said as I looked for a way through the rocks that were suddenly dotting the channel. "We're in a different world here, pal."

"What do you mean?" Max asked, his smile evaporating.

"There's too much current here; we're dropping too fast. We just barely made it around those jams and sweepers. I didn't expect there to be so much water."

"Oh," Max said, looking around as though there were threats everywhere.

At the end of a straight stretch about a quarter mile long, the river headed into a sandstone wall, waves building as they crashed into the wall. There was a hard left-hand turn to be made partway through the rapid, which meant we had to turn sideways to paddle to the left and skirt the wall. We handled it, but something wasn't right. I tried to remember what Dr. Vacation had said: "Nothing but some ripples and waves, except for a pretty good one midway through the canyon, and the big one at the end. You might want to scout that one. You can run them fine if you've got some experience."

They'd had three rafts, he said; how would this section have looked if there were three rafts instead of one, ten people instead of two? Another raft would have made a difference, certainly: two people on one raft this far away from any hope of rescue are pretty vulnerable. And if his rafts had been larger than the *Dunny*, they might have flattened out the waves. But mostly the water had been lower when he went, because the snowpack was gone and there was less meltwater off the glaciers. Our mid-July river was higher than a September one.

In fact, we were on a different river from the one Dr. Vacation had seen. We were alone, a single small raft with no other support, on a river that might have twice, three times as much volume as on the good doctor's trip. A different river.

The Sheslay showed no sign of slowing; it was as though we were accelerating down a slope. Soon we came to another turn, where the waves formed on the left, then swept around to the right, behind a gravel bar filled with young alders that blocked our view of what lay downstream.

"This looks interesting," Max said. All I could see were the waves growing steadily larger, and none of the run-out. "We'd better scout it," I said. "Let's paddle over to that eddy there." I pointed at a tiny eddy on the inside of the right turn.

"You think we need to?" Max asked, looking skeptically at what appeared to be mild waves, a pleasant rolling ride.

"I can't tell what's around the corner, and we don't want to get into it and find some monster hole when it's too late."

"I guess so." Max shrugged. "But it doesn't look like much from here." Sometimes I could let the raft swing wide and take a look to know the run was okay, then get Max to paddle frantically back into the main current and ride the waves. But other corners were too acute and there was no way to see around them, so we hopscotched from one side of the river to the other, trying to see around corners or catching eddies.

When we found an eddy, I would jog down the bar to take a look, while Max stood on shore, holding the *Dunny* by its bow line. Sometimes I was glad we scouted: the river was swelling from side streams, and it seemed to be dropping faster, too. The waves got higher, the holes deeper.

"Major hole on the left," I reported to Max after one such scout.

"Can we run it?" he asked.

"Probably, but let's not."

"Why? It might be fun."

"We'll catch the edge of it if you want, but we're starting to get to the limits of the *Dunny* for this sort of thing."

"Limits? What limits?" Max asked, squatting on a rock, still holding to the *Dunny* by its line, like a cowboy holding the reins of his horse.

"The raft can handle big waves—it's been down the Grand Canyon. But that's when it's running waves straight on. When you have to maneuver in a rapid, you're turned sideways, and that means you can flip, because you're exposing the short side to the wave. We're not there yet, but the waves keep getting bigger, don't they?"

Max didn't answer. "Man," he said, "I'm getting tired."

I was, too. This constant scouting and the muscling back and forth across currents to catch eddies or to avoid a wall were draining. There were no stretches where we could pause for a moment, put down the paddle, and check out the canyon. The distance between one turn and the next was sometimes no more than a hundred yards. The river was too fast and too constant for pauses.

We got back into the raft and pushed off. We bent around to the right, found the biggest wave, and rode its edge. It was a nice ride, but when we came down from the crest, there was another wall dead ahead, with another extreme left-hand turn. This time, though, the waves went straight into the wall before making a ninety-degree cut to the left. Much of the water couldn't make the turn but fell into whipping whirlpools on each side, with the one on the right frothing.

If we rode the waves in too far, we would get broadsided against the wall and flip. We couldn't allow ourselves to slip off to the right, either, as the whirlpool looked strong enough to flip us there, too.

It was too late to stop. "Damn, we'll have to go," I said in a rush. "We'll run down the center and turn to the left. If we go up on the wall, it'll be on your side, and we'll have to climb that tube. We don't want to fall off into the pool on the right."

Max had gotten over saying "This looks interesting" at every rapid and had substituted "Oh shit" instead. "Oh shit," he said.

Then we were cascading, tumbling down the rumbling waves, over the broad washboard that narrowed and led to the wall. "Back," I ordered, trying to slow our rocket down. "Make a left," I added a second later. Max paddled hard ahead and I pulled back, to swing the bow toward the left. "Now—" I paused, waiting for the right moment. But I waited a beat too long. "—Go!" But we were already washing sideways toward the wall. We paddled as hard as we could, but it had no effect; we started to plaster on the wall. "Go high," I yelled. "Paddle," I added, confusing matters.

Max scrambled onto his tube as the raft surged up on the stone. His side went high and I slid across from my tube toward Max's while my tube was sucked low by the boiling waters beneath the raft. We were poised for a moment, in that delicious second between the correct position and disaster: upside down.

Slowly the boat came down from the wall. We fell back onto our tubes; adrenaline took over, and we paddled frantically downstream for no reason.

"Fuck, man," I said, when we slowed ourselves enough to stop paddling.

"Jehesus!" Max yelled, drawing out the word to three syllables. "Jesus," he said again, only two syllables this time.

I reached for our bail bucket and hauled water out of the *Dunny*—a lot of water. "That was close, man," I sputtered, "close." I tried to make it sound as though I had enjoyed the thrill of it, but really I was shaken: not so much by that particular rapid but by its implications. I stopped bailing then, because another turn was coming up and we needed to paddle.

Fortunately these rapids didn't have many rocks. The Sheslay, in July, was mostly waves and walls, although I searched for holes, the sudden, foaming pits that are created when a large-enough rock in a steep-enough section of river is covered by water. Given the volume of water in the river now, if we were to run a hole, it would likely flip us. This was one of those things I didn't have to think about; the knowledge was there, I hadn't lost it—a river guide's automatic awareness of the river.

The afternoon passed, but to us, the day was just water and river and canyon. I didn't look at the sky or at any of the sights downstream and took only a glance or two at the bluffs to read the turns of the river. Every corner was a decision—run it or not?—and every scout was draining: stumbling over the boulders, examining the rapid in the glare of the afternoon sun, then walking back across the gravel bar, explaining the rapid to Max, and shoving off again, paddling hard to get ourselves out of the eddy and into the approach to the run.

Turn after turn after turn—the right turns in particular consistent, for the river seemed to want to head east but kept encountering obdurate walls which prevented that, so the river smashed into those walls and bent back to the north and west, then tried its assault again farther on.

We came to another corner, where the waves entering the turn were the biggest so far. As we paddled down on it and slid out to the left, we could see a very big wave, coupled with a frothing something just beyond it. That froth could be either a breaking part of a wave, or a hole. Bad enough if it were a breaking wave, much worse if a hole.

"We've got to stop again," I said.

Max groaned, still paddling. "Again? Jesus," he sighed.

I took a glance at him as we brought the raft into a skinny little eddy on the left shore. His face was beaded with sweat, and his brow was deeply furrowed, as though he would never lose those furrows again. I could feel my own permanent furrows etched into my face from the squinting.

"We need to find a camp," I said. "Let's get up on top of this ridge and walk down to that point. We can scout this and look for a camp. And I think we'd better get a look at what's downstream. Dr. Vacation said when there got to be straight bluffs on both sides like this, then the first major rapid was close. I don't want to get surprised by that one."

Max flopped back on the tube. "Man, I'm really, totally wasted now," he said.

"Me, too." I nodded, remaining with him on the tube. "This is wild."

"Yeah," Max agreed, sitting up. "Let's find camp."

We tied the raft and began doing battle with the brush and rock of the bluff. The bluff was laced with the scooped washes of old creeks, and each creek bottom was choked with trees, tree debris, vines, and bushes. We stepped deep into a pile, then lifted ourselves up onto a log, then fell off of that into a thorny bush, then tried to find our way around another particularly vicious pile.

A few yards after we reached the top of the bluff—about a hundred feet above the river—we could see that we had made a rare wise decision. All of the water on this right turn was pushing to the left, and on the left was that wave we had seen and a growling hole below it: a huge hole, a flip hole, maybe six feet from crest to bottom. Lucky thing we had stopped— once we came around the corner, we would have had fifty feet to spot the foam and avoid it. We wouldn't have.

Immediately after the hole was another one of those walls, this one worse than any other: the water didn't just hit the wall but built up on it, layers of water slamming into it, then spinning off to the left, with a whirlpool and eddy on the right.

"How's that look?" Max asked, hopefully.

"Screwed," I said. "I can't believe this shit."

"Can we do it?" he asked. I had a moment of sympathy for him—he wasn't able to judge the severity of the rapids we encountered, and so he had to depend upon me to tell him about them.

"We can do it, I think, but who knows what's around the corner."

"Maybe we should go look," he suggested.

Max led on. We stomped and kicked our way through the brush, until we came out on the headland at the point where the river turned left. The vigor of the wall-smash was clearer from here; the water seemed to be climbing the wall, as though it were trying to escape the canyon. There was a possible camp on the shore opposite us, a tiny sand beach at the end of an island. It wouldn't be an easy beach to catch, and getting back out into the current tomorrow to position ourselves properly for the wall run would be difficult, but since we'd entered the Sheslay canyon, there hadn't been many beaches, and it was late.

As long as we were up here, we needed to find out one other thing. We crawled a few more yards on our bellies, across moss and out as close to the edge of the bluff as we dared, since the bluff was undercut, hanging unsupported over the river.

Creeping out, we peered downstream. The river ran straight and smooth for a quarter mile or so, as clean and straight as an arrow. Then it ended.

"Oh my . . ."

"What?"

"Goddamn it . . ."

"What? What is it?"

I sighed loudly. "Nothing. Just a big, black cave."

"Oh. That sounds interesting. What do we do?" Max asked.

"Stop. Camp," I said. "Worry about it tomorrow."

The lovely smooth stretch of river downstream ended at two short, perfectly vertical walls. The river made a sharp turn to the right between the walls and disappeared. All we could see between the walls was spray; spray and mist and water being shot high into the air. We could hear it, a rumbling in the tight canyon, the sound made by water pouring over rocks and into foaming, boiling, nasty holes.

"Is that it?" Max asked. "The first one?"

"You bet," I said, confident for once of where we were.

We beat our way back to the boat, our spirits somehow lifted. Perhaps it was the pleasure of knowing where we were. It was late afternoon; shadows stretched across the Sheslay, yet the sun glinted viciously off the waves. We slid down the lower part of the bluff into the eddy where the *Dunny* rode, its stern bobbing far too jauntily in the eddy. I went over the run with Max: "We'll make a right turn leaving this eddy, power hard over to that side, straighten out for the waves, ride the right edge of the hole, then make another right and catch that eddy we saw low on the right. If it looks like we can't make the eddy, I'll call a left, and we'll run the wall and try to camp around the corner; got it?" "Got it," said Max, but I had my doubts.

"Here we go," I said, and the river grabbed us for a minute, taking us too far downstream on the left before our cross-river paddling took effect and we cut across to the right. As we came around the corner, the wave and hole exploded into view, lit by the low sun and the roaring thunder of the water pouring over the rock and into the hole.

Max matched me stroke for stroke, and we cleared the hole. As we passed, I glanced over at it: a frothing, foaming, roaring monster's mouth of a hole. Then we were sliding, bouncing down the bony side of the rapid, over barely submerged rocks, and we plopped with a smack into the upper end of an eddy alongside the island.

We dragged the *Dunny* up on the even, round, river rocks of the beach-cum-gravel bar that would be home. After we unloaded it and tied it down, we sat on the tubes, lamenting our situation.

"Why didn't I pay attention?"

"What am I doing here?"

"What do we do if we can't run it?" Max finally asked, slipping off the tube and onto the soft, warm sand.

"We can portage, probably," I said, although having seen those walls, I wasn't sure we could. "What worries me is that we might find bigger stuff downstream—how do I know?—and we'll be over our heads if we do; if that happens, we might have to find a way to get out of here," I concluded, looking around me at the canyon walls to the east and west.

"Great," said Max.

"Problem is," I added, "I don't know where we'd hike to. I don't think there's anything much that way," indicating the northeast rim with my finger, "and I know there's nothing that way," pointing to the southwest, where there were nothing but mountains and glaciers and rivers all the way to the coast. "But we could probably hike down to the confluence, where that cabin is supposed to be."

"We're not walking out of here," Max said firmly. "No way."

"Well, then, we'll just have to run it. It's kind of fun, though," I ventured.

"Yeah, it is," Max agreed, prone on the sand, eyes closed. "I just wish I knew what the big one was going to be like."

"Me, too. Guess we'll find out tomorrow."

"Guess so," Max agreed.

Eventually Max lifted himself out of the sand and continued whittling on the spoon he'd been making for me. Being on land helped me regain my balance. The river had surprised me, and I hadn't adjusted well. Standing on shore I could see it rightly. If the rapids continued to get harder, we would be in trouble; we were at the edge, the edge of what two men alone could handle. But the rapids we had run so far had been manageable, thrilling. If today had been the end of our run, if there were no downstream to confront, then we would have had a splendid day, if a bit tense. This wasn't like running the Tuolumne blind or the Middle Fork in high water, wasn't like the time I ran the upper Stanislaus at midnight, under a full moon. Still, it was dumb, I said to myself, dumb to be out here with one boat and just two of us; dumb not to have paid better attention to Dr. Vacation; dumb not to have considered the possibility that the river would be like this. Still, the *Oyster Dunny* was holding up magnificently. It had been as tight as a banker's heart all day. At least I could still patch a raft. Although, given its age and condition, it could explode tomorrow and leave us helpless.

As evening came on, I relaxed, slipped further into the mood of the place. The wall fifty yards from us still looked ugly, but it was only river, water, rapids—this was the sort of thing I had known for a long time. And after all, it was what I had wanted: something difficult, like Sid at Miles Canyon.

This was also a beautiful place to be. Our slip of a gravel bar seemed like a delicate, bonsai version of a camp. Directly downstream was a bare tan bluff that rose straight up a hundred feet or so. On top of it was a picket line of trees—some standing, some falling—and back of that a half mile was the higher ridge of the canyon, a dry, green mix of rock and trees.

On the main shore across from our island, a shady copse grew. It was a grotto, a sylvan retreat. I gazed at that and at the river rushing past, and things didn't seem so bad. The sky, which had been blank all day, stayed that way through the evening. The Sheslay pounded past, incredibly loud when I took the time to notice the sound. I walked up the bar, to where our island started. Along with creek water running beneath ferns, this is one of the great views on rivers: bare stones, white and gray, meeting a frantic rush of water, also white and gray. The clash of stolid and passionate.

After dinner we tried an experiment. The river was moving nearly as fast as such a notoriously speedy place as Lava Falls in Grand Canyon or even Telegraph Creek on the Stikine. I wanted to see how fast that fast was, so I stepped off thirty feet along the rocky bank of our camp and placed Max at the lower end. I tossed a heavy stick into the water upstream of us, and when it crossed my mark, I yelled to Max, who started the stopwatch on his wristwatch. Max clocked the stick at 3.48 seconds for the thirty feet, and I did the math. Thirty feet is 1/176th of a mile, and 176 multiplied by 3.48 seconds equals 616 seconds, roughly, which means that the stick would have traveled a mile in 10 minutes and 16 seconds, a rate just a touch slower than six miles an hour. That didn't seem as fast as the river looked, but the stick was obviously lagging behind the true rate of the current. The river was probably running about seven or eight miles per hour, very fast for a river.

That night while we sat in the sand, leaning against the *Dunny* and staring into the fire, Max handed me the spoon. "Here it is," he said. He'd been working on it for a week. It was five inches long, made out of a cottonwood branch, and the handle was wrapped in thread from the raft-patching kit. I'd adapted to not having a spoon long before, but I was touched by the gift, and vowed to keep it. "Thanks, man," I told him. "I'll try to keep you from drowning tomorrow."

Max smiled. "That would be nice." I thought he would say something about male gratitude, about how men take care of one another, but that sort of thing seemed to have ended back on the Chutine, around Barrington Mountain.

We listened to the fire crackle some more. "Beautiful, ain't it?" I said.

Max sighed. He looked up at the smoke rising into the stars. "I guess this is what you came for, a place like this?"

"I suppose so. I didn't figure it would be just this way, but that's okay. It's a river. Is this what you imagined when you were sitting on Denny's couch?"

"I'm alright," he replied. This didn't seem like an answer.

"Hey, I just noticed how quiet you've been lately."

He giggled and pushed his glasses higher on his nose. The fire reflected off them, and he lifted a handful of sand and let it spill out between his fingers. "Other things on my mind."

There were only two of us on the Sheslay and one aging raft, and the river had turned difficult. In a way I was even farther from home and wife here than I'd been on the Chutine. Still, it was okay to be here. All I heard was the river and fire. Perhaps this was the source of my contentment in our lonely camp—the absence of a voice warning me about the morning.

Max and I talked a little about the next day. Not long before we went to our bags, a bull moose appeared silently out of the grotto on shore, as though he'd sprung directly from the brow of the hill behind him. He moseyed toward us a ways, then lifted his head and saw us. He pawed the ground a little, shook his rack at us, walked a few feet toward us, then stopped and retreated in a way that could only be taken as sullen.

I looked around at the bar and realized we were on a natural path between the lower and upper ends of it. The moose's manner suggested that he wanted to go where we were: twisting his head, stamping his feet, advancing upon us, then withdrawing. As it grew dark, the standoff continued, not that I was tempted to move—given our other issues, a cranky moose didn't command too much concern.

"I don't like the way he's acting," Max said.

"What can he do?" I asked with a shrug. "Trample us?"

"Yes. Exactly," Max said bitterly. "That's exactly what he could do."

"I don't think he will," I said, looking at the river again, trying to get a feel for the speed of it.

When it became too dark to see the moose, although we could still hear him feeding, we gave up on the night. We built the fire high and went to bed. I assumed that with the assortment of guilts and regrets weighing on me, with the moose and the rapid and tomorrow, I'd fret a while in my bag. As usual, though, I barely had time to consider our plight before I was asleep.

Opening my eyes I realized I was smelling water: the smell of a rapid. I heard it, too, and could feel it through the sand, through my sleeping bag and my back. As though I were a part of the Sheslay. How many times had I awakened next to a river; how familiar were these sensations? There was nothing strange about them. I would get up, gather my gear, and run the river. An ordinary day—if I were twenty-two and single.

The first thing I noticed was the perfect day: clear, a crisp edge, breathless. The second thing was the moose prints leading across the channel to our island. The bull had walked right into camp during the night: across the back channel, up our beach, and within six feet of the fire pit. I was amazed both by his chutzpah and by the fact that we hadn't heard him, a moose Ahab, monomaniacal pursuer of his destiny.

After I told Max, and he had stumbled around for a while in that stunned, somnambulant condition he had in the morning, he announced his revelation. "I've got it," he said.

"Oh yeah? What?" I asked, expecting to hear a wildlife biologist's lecture on climate, temperature, rutting season, dominance display.

Max just pointed. At the *Oyster Dunny*. At the moose rack still roped high on the bow. To a nearsighted moose it might have looked like a friendly face.

The river seemed less loud. The water had dropped a little, but mostly the river was quieter because it was morning, and after several cups of coffee we were brave, fearless. "Are we ready?" Max asked when the gear was tied.

We did some twisting and bending and stretching, warming up. We spun the *Dunny* around so the nose was pointed into the current and upstream. I rolled up the stern line, asked Max if he was okay.

"Okay," he said, looking downstream, sounding ill.

I gave one hard push, then jumped onto the rear tube and ran a few steps along it to my spot. "Here we go!" I warned.

We shot into the center of the river, spun to the downstream angle, and waited as we rode the middle of the current down into the eye of the morning's maelstrom.

Only as a memory was I conscious of this: the lift and drop of the raft in the waves; the splashes off the tubes; the morning sun flashing on the waves; the roar of the water amplified by the wall—we descended on the wall, drawn toward it as if pulled by a string. Down and up, twisting side to side, building—more waves, more light, more sound, until it is an explosion of sound and sight, too much to separate.

Some runs are so perfect, they are like a favorite melody, whose notes are expected, but moving anyway. We were that perfect. We rode up high on the wall, no more than six inches closer to it than I wanted, and dropped forward into the current at just the right moment. It was a dream run, over too soon.

"All right!" I whooped.

"That was excellent," said Max. "Now what do we do?"

I wanted to savor our triumph, but Max was right, we needed to think about what was next. We bobbed into shore about fifty yards upstream of the black canyon downstream, and in tandem we leapt out of the boat to secure it. We scrambled through the underbrush to the dark wall that rose from the river. We huffed and puffed our way to the top, to a ridge of crumbling rock, and looked down—into dismal beauty.

It was like a microcosm of all rapids, every rapid, as though someone had laid out the perfect obstacle course: rocks, holes, waves, walls. The river was corseted by the tiny canyon, and the hundred-by-twenty-five-yard section was filled with white, with waves, with roaring. At first there seemed to be no path through them all. "My goodness," I said.

It was a beautiful stretch, with smooth, clean entry waves, the pure green of the water spilling over into deep holes, then rising up to cresting waves that broke back upstream in a frothy white, over and over again, pounding and shuddering when they did, a pounding that we could feel where we stood. All of the river then rushed against the black wall on the opposite side, before opening into a broad pool and disappearing downstream around another bend.

The main problem was a monster hole on the right-hand side toward the top of the canyon. There was no way I wanted any part of that. But if we ran to the left of it, we would have a hard time staying off the black wall, and the waves were crashing into that wall, and just downstream of that were two steep waves, about six or seven feet tall, that needed to be run head-on.

We worked our way up and down the ridge, trying to find the line. As I looked at the canyon, my guide's mind plotted routes, rejected and embraced them, amended, hypothesized, and assumed things about each. Every move had a problem; no run was clean.

There was nothing to do but read and read and read the water, and let the path reveal itself. I was alone in this: Max didn't have the skills to help, and he had stopped trying after a few minutes, sitting on the moss on top of the bluff looking glum.

Once I had figured out the run, I imagined mistakes and tried to deal with them. Then I went over the line until I had it memorized, until I could visualize exactly how it would go. Max waited for me, pulling up patches of moss and tossing them off the bluff into the roaring.

"Okay, here it is," I said, plopping down beside him. "The big hole?" I asked, pointing. Max nodded. "That's our first and biggest problem. We don't want to go in there no matter what. So I'm thinking we'll ride just to the left of it, on top of that hump there; then we've got the next problem. See how that water hits the wall?"

"Yep," said Max, breathlessly, as though he didn't have enough oxygen in his lungs to speak.

"Well, we don't want to hit that wall. But we don't want to make a right turn either and try to paddle away, because that would mean going into the wall sideways, and we'd dump for sure if that happened."

"So what do we do?"

"I think," I continued, "that when we come off the hump, and go into that trough, we'll get slowed down enough to back-paddle away from the wall, then do a turn at the last second to take those ugly waves against the wall bow first."

"What happens if we don't?"

"You'll need to remember to climb the high side of the raft," I told him. "If we go into the wall we'll hit on my side, so remember, go to my side. Don't ever stop paddling unless I tell you to, and keep the high side in mind. Even a little shift can make a difference."

Max nodded, and we came down from the ridge. We retied the raft, tightening all lines and hiding anything that would hit us in a flip. I untied us and nudged the raft free from the sand. We drifted about ten feet to a place that showed me the perfect line for the run: if we went straight from there, we would make it. It was as though a mist had cleared and everything downstream was obvious. The run was clear, what it would do to the raft seemed certain, and the result would be perfect. Before I could lose this feeling I said, "I see it, let's go," and we began.

We paddled closer. "Splash your face," I told Max.

"What?" he asked, not taking his eyes from the drop.

"Splash your face. It'll get you ready, keep the water from shocking you," I said as I reached over for a handful of water to throw on my face. "And yell. Whoop, holler; it helps."

Max took a few fingers of water and tapped them toward his face. The whitewater looked worse than it had from the bluff, now that we were in smelling distance of it, could feel the spray of it blowing back upstream.

I yelled something as we reached the lip of the first smooth wave. Max whooped. As with all big rapids, this one slowed time: it unspooled slowly, giving us a chance to experience, intensely, what was happening. We rode up on the hump we had aimed for, but a touch farther left than I had hoped. I couldn't do anything about it, so we slid down into the trough. As I'd expected, we slowed.

We pulled back hard, trying to keep clear of the wall, but although the trough had slowed us, the force of the water was stronger than I had thought, and we were pushed into the wall. Finally it was too late; we had to make the turn to face the downstream waves. Max back-paddled, I stroked forward, bracing for our descent into the troughs.

The troughs were big, and the waves tall, and together they thrashed us. Both Max and I ended up in the center of the raft for a moment, falling off the tubes into a pool of cold water and onto each other, then lurching back up as the raft reared and twisted and the river roared. It was loud in there, as loud as I've ever heard a rapid, all the sound reflecting off the wall. In seconds it was over, although every moment was so distinct it seemed to be many moments—millions of them.

Then we were out, soaking wet, huffing, ecstatic. We had no time to celebrate, since we were bearing down on an island, but we allowed ourselves an extra whoop and a holler. "Wahoo," Max offered, ceremonially.

Then we made a left, went past the island, and eddied out below. Such a pure high, a lovely emotional moment, when one has passed a big rapid. Even better if it has been done with grace: we had found a good line through a rapid that didn't have many.

We stayed in the eddy below the island, bailing the boat and reliving the run, with smiles. The dry mouths and tight lips of an hour before were gone.

———

"Nasty place," I offered.

"That was wild," said Max. "How did that rate? Compared to other rapids?"

"That was a good one; like a mix of the hole at Clavey and the run at Cliffside, but a lot bigger waves than Cliffside. That was fun, man, that was the real thing. I thought we were in a washing machine, the way we were getting worked."

"And it wasn't even the Big One." Max scooped another bucket of water out of the raft.

"That's right." I stopped bailing for a minute. "If that wasn't the big one, imagine what the big one will be like."

Max didn't answer, pondering the image of this larger rapid.

"The *Dunny* came through, didn't she?" I said admiringly.

"Good old boat." Max drummed her tubes a few times, and she made a pleased boing.

Black Wall Falls, the boring name we settled on for the canyon, marked a turning point. It was as though the river had been building to that climax, then, having been compressed between those two walls, spilled over into a new thing. Throughout the rest of the morning, the river was consistent. As before, there were right-hand turns that were sweeping and gradual, followed by radical left turns where the water piled into walls with eddies or boils on either side. Only now they weren't steadily getting worse.

For the next five miles we worked constantly, moving to the outside of turns and back across, trying to avoid eddying out. There was no such thing as a straight, no section where we could pause and notice things. It was a marathon, not a sprint—there were no pools to drop into but only swift water in between screaming turns.

"How you doing, man?" Max asked.

"Good, good," I said, keeping my eye on the river ahead. "How about you?"

"I'm fine," Max answered, sounding as though he were surprised to discover this.

Occasionally I would try to look up, lift my eyes above the nearby bluffs to check the canyon for sign of a tributary coming in from the right. That would be the mark of the last rapid, the big one, the dividing line between the Sheslay and the more pacific Nahlin and Inklin run. But it didn't show.

We stopped for lunch, muscles aching. The day, which had started out bright, clouded over, and we traveled in shadow, with a strong wind gusting at times. It felt as though a front was moving in. After lunch we headed back into the twists of the river, each twist similar to the one before and the one after. After an hour or so, a change happened. The rapids eased. I checked my map—still trying—and saw that near the confluence the canyon wall to our right would start to give way. This seemed to be happening now, a rare correspondence between the map and the river. The confluence had to be—had to be—coming up.

In late afternoon we headed into a long left-hand turn. Nothing about it looked particularly threatening, but we stopped on the right anyhow. I left the tied-up raft with Max and climbed onto a flat, aspen-covered plateau. As I walked I gradually became aware of another canyon appearing on the other side of the plateau. Then, as I looked farther to my right and caught sight of a river, I realized there was something unnatural over there —a structure, a cabin. The cabin and the river meant we had arrived: the Nahlin. If that was the Nahlin, I reasoned, then here—I swung my head back to the Sheslay—must be the Big One. And there it was.

A straight line all the way across the river, marking a drop of about eight feet. From right to left were a huge logjam, then a large reversing wave, then a foaming hole, and somewhere on the left, the hope of a run.

There wasn't any doubt: this was it, and it looked bad. I went back upstream and hollered at Max. "This is it!"

Max shot up from his supine position. I waved at him. "Come on."

He scrambled out of the raft and up the slope of the ridge. "We're there, man," I told him. "I saw the cabin across the way and then I saw the falls— it looks hairy."

We walked along the flat ridge to where the ridge narrowed, as it separated the Sheslay from the Nahlin, and down next to the logjam on the Sheslay. The jam, which extended thirty yards from shore and about another thirty from upstream to down-, took up a third of the river. There was a bald eagle sitting on top of the pile, looking regal, even though he was just waiting for something to die. He flew off the pile and into the dead branches of a tree on shore.

We scrambled around on the logs, changing perspective, trying different angles, and drawing conclusions. There was no way through on this side. Beyond the logjam was a sheer drop into a foaming pit of bubbles: impossible. Next to that were two tall pour-overs, separated by water humping over a rock that would force us either into the right or the left pour-over. Beyond those was a tongue of relatively smooth water, and past that, on the far left shore, was another horrendous pour-over.

"Nothing over here," I said to Max. I pointed out our one shot. "That tongue over there? I think that's the run. Or at least it's the only one I see. Let's go take a look from that side."

Quiet again, we retraced our steps. We had to pull the raft upstream as far as we could, to have enough time to paddle across to the left shore before being swept over the falls. We made it—panting—and tied up the *Dunny*, then walked slowly down along the shore, reading the approach.

The falls were formed by a ledge that shot up out of the ground on this side and continued all the way across the river. We followed the ledge right out into the river to get a good, clean look at the falls.

"Wow," Max said, turning to me for insight as we stood on the ledge.

I just looked, back and forth, up and down the rapid. There was only the one possible place to go, about fifteen feet from shore. The tongue led to a wave that was a good eight to ten feet high and seemed to be straight up and down. The pour-overs on either side of the tongue looked like accidents waiting to happen. But if we could get lined up right on that tongue, we would be in decent shape. Not perfect: the tongue was mottled by currents coming from many directions. And the tongue itself went too deep, and the downstream crest of the wave was breaking back, which is no good, since you can have a perfect run into such a wave, then be beaten back by a crest that hits you at the wrong moment. I tried counting the beats, to get a fix on how often this wave broke, but even the timing of its breaks was irregular.

The other obstacle was a car-sized rock upstream, shaped in a rough V. My plan when I first saw the run was to go to the left of that rock, then work our way back to the right slightly. The danger was that the waves coming off the rock would force us too much to the left and into the pour-over next to shore.

The river was moving so fast and with such force that I wasn't sure what I was seeing. I thought I was seeing a run, and a few moves that would have to be made. My eye told me this was a clean run; my head offered other possibilities. The only solution to the conflict between eye and head was to keep looking and, oddly enough, listening.

Over the years a voice has occasionally made itself heard when I am on a river. A voice that is not a voice, but the river itself. Most guides have had a similar experience, which is a form of reading water that involves simply listening to the river. This happens when you look at a rapid long enough so that it seems to be telling you something, although what it is telling you is usually an either/or: either this will go, it says, or this won't.

I listened for that voice, that whisper from the river. The voice would supersede both eye and head and would offer the truest word I was likely to get. I listened for that voice, while Max talked, and I stared.

The scouting went on and on. Each time I passed my eye over the run, it became clearer, and the river's voice became stronger, but not strong enough, so I looked and listened some more. Finally as we squatted there on the ledge beside the falls, Max nudged me and said, dramatically, "Let's do it," with a smile.

I smiled back, at his melodramatic tone more than anything else. I looked a few more times at the water and thought I had heard all that it was going to tell me, so I nodded.

We walked back upstream, staying close to shore. I turned around every few feet to check the line, to burn it into memory so I would know what to expect at every moment. We went past the big rock, and I noted its breaking waves once again, trying to understand them. The run felt right. The eagle was still perched on a dead snag across the river, watching us.

Back at the *Dunny* we retied the gear. No matter how confident I was of the run, it was clearly a bad one. We probably could make the run without flipping or coming out of the boat. In other circumstances that might have been enough; but the cabin across the way was obviously deserted, and in addition to getting injured falling out of the raft—never mind drowning—there were other problems, such as losing the raft or being so fatigued by the swim that we wouldn't be able to care for ourselves. The thought of flipping by itself didn't trouble me too much; the idea of dealing with the aftermath of a flip troubled me a lot.

After we were tied down, I told Max I wanted to go look at the rapid one more time, to be sure of the run.

He looked stricken. He had strapped his climbing helmet on and had cinched his life jacket as tight as he could get it. He was completely wired. He had made himself have no questions or doubts, no hesitation. Making him wait reintroduced doubt. But on the river I was in charge, so he had no choice, and I began retracing my steps along the shore. I was only checking my line; I wanted to give my brain one more chance to absorb the rapid and to understand the approach.

I had been hearing so many other voices in the silence of that hard country that it should have been no surprise to hear one more. But I was surprised; I hadn't heard this one before, and as I walked, it asked a simple question. That question was, "Is this necessary?"

I recognized the voice. It was the voice of Pat, my wife. As I walked on, the question repeated. It was so clear I almost looked around, as though my very-pregnant wife had somehow materialized out there. I didn't answer, but I knew what the question meant: that I hadn't asked myself a number of questions about this, including whether running the falls was really necessary. This was my guilt speaking—pure, naked guilt for the selfishness of this trip.

I'd been ignoring it for days, and now I couldn't anymore. This was stupid, the whole thing was stupid. I wasn't a guide anymore; I was a professor, a father—I had no business being here, risking my neck for no reason. My mother-in-law was dying, my wife was in pain, who knew how the baby was doing? The older children, barely teenagers, were having to take care of their mother while I was here trying to decide such weighty matters as, Should I run a particular rapid or not? It was an indulgence, an embarrassment, and I was ashamed. I broke out in a sweat and walked on.

It would compound the foolishness to take this risk now, unnecessarily, in this faux adventure. I had felt a debt to Sid, to pay homage to him and to the power of rivers. What I owed my wife I hadn't considered. Her voice hadn't been asking me to consider that—it was only asking a simple question, an honest question, being curious.

I got right down to the ledge where the falls formed, and I squatted beside the river and looked into it. Nothing. Then I looked at the breaking wave and I looked at it and looked, and eventually I heard something, although all I heard were numbers. Four out of ten. If we ran it ten times, we'd flip or wash out four times. I knew that as a fact, as certain as anything could be. Were those good odds?

The answer from the river, from everywhere, was clear. No, they weren't, and none of this was necessary.

So I went back. I should have been more disappointed than I was. This was the last chance I had to meet Sid, to do something in my river life that would match his. Ever since I'd stopped in Wrangell on my way back from the Noatak six years before, I had been looking for a moment like this. To let go of the moment was to let go of the silly, vague, but real desire to add to the family river legacy.

When I came back to the *Dunny*, Max was lying on one tube with his helmet on, eyes closed, as mournful as a beaten dog. I walked up and said, "We're not going."

He sat up. "What? Why not?" He meant to invest the question with outrage, but it didn't work. He wasn't outraged; he was relieved, although he was also puzzled.

I told him the story then, about how I had heard my wife's voice, and how I had listened to the river to decide whether we could go or not. I don't think Max minded too much, although he said he had really let himself go this time, deciding that he would follow me on the rapid, despite what appeared to him to be an ugly, ugly falls. That was the only time I felt sorry — it is a bad thing to rob someone of new experiences.

Max got a peaceful look in his eye and told a long, unclear story about having had a waking dream while I was gone, where there was a wolf, a dog, and a coyote. Coyote was the one Max admired, because he had said he would be clever and survive. While I didn't follow the tale too well, I got the point: it was okay to be clever and survive, rather than holding fast to some false ideal that missed the main goal: the idea is to survive.

We untied the *Dunny* and cast off, silent as sphinxes. The air had come out of the day like a sigh. We would slide downstream as close as we could get, and begin our portage. We drifted around the corner, and there it was — a horizontal line, where the river entirely disappeared. If we kept drifting, we would disappear with it. All we had to do was keep floating, then make the right moves about fifty yards downstream.

———

"Hey Max," I could have said.

"What?" he might have answered.

"Let's go."

"What?!" More sharply this time.

"Let's do it."

"Run it?"

"Yeah."

"Now?"

"Yeah."

"Well . . ." and I was pretty sure that the very next thing he would have said was, "Okay."

———

There is nothing very interesting about a portage—it is simply lugging gear over difficult ground and reassembling it again somewhere else. It took us more than an hour to get the gear down a steep slope just beyond the broad ledge that made the rapid. There was a small, deep pool on the downstream side of the ledge, and Max rigged up a pulley system using the climbing ropes and carabiners, and together we lowered the gear to the river. It was an ugly perch at riverside, with nothing but sharp-edged slate to stand or rest gear on. I worried about inflating the *Dunny* on such a prickly place, but it was late by then, a very long day behind us, and I was too tired to care very much—I could always patch the raft again.

We inflated the raft, tossed our stuff into the bottom of it, and shoved off, taking a last look at the foaming falls. For a moment I saw it from two perspectives: from a river pilot's of the turn of the century, coming upstream and finding this impassible barrier; and from the perspective of myself as a younger man, traveling with a group of guides, when it would have been great fun to come across such a place. The perspectives had this in common, that they were not the one I had at that moment or ever would have again. My own perspective was a muddle, somewhere in between seeing the falls as impossible or as exhilarating; this vision lasted only a moment, though, because sooner or later you must turn downriver and see what is coming next . . .

———

And this is the way I wanted it to be:

Though I shouldn't be, suddenly I am glad. I knew this means that I am a bad person, a rotten husband, and I am probably going to hell—but here is a rapid and I am a guide.

"We'll swing around to the left of this rock, angle right, and we'll power hard forward. When we go in, dive toward the front."

He doesn't speak. He shifts about on the tube, screwing himself firmly into place.

I let us slide with the current. Thirty feet. We float in perfect position, approaching the left side of the rock. I try to read the force of the waves surging off the rock, to figure out when to make our move. Twenty feet. "One stroke," I call. We need to be closer to the rock but not so close that the surge will push us left. Fifteen feet. "Another."

I want us to be early rather than late, but I still wait another beat. Twelve. "Now—stroke easy," and we start. The bow of the raft, angled right, noses into the first surges but we hold our position; into the next ones and I can feel the water pushing us back, wrong, left. "Go harder," I say, my voice rising. He reaches in.

Then we are there, at the edge of a canyon of water—no more timing, no more strategy. I yell, and I reach as far out of the raft as I can, take the strongest stroke I can. Leaning out I see the wave a few feet ahead, can feel it, even, a wind generated by it, can taste the mist of it. We struggle with the currents; we are holding position, then losing, then "GO! GO! GO!" I bellow with each of our strokes, and we begin to beat the current and edge to the right. We will have to twist any second to face downstream. We can't go in sideways—we'd flip in an instant. "GO!"

One more stroke, two more, and I switch and back-paddle, jamming the paddle into the water and leaning back on it for a moment as the bow swings slowly to the left, straight downstream. Then I reach forward into the water dropping away from me.

We plunge down, into a hole that is too deep to come out of. When the bow of the raft starts to come up, we both reach for a stroke again, this time reaching up at the water over our heads, and I think we fall back as the raft rears up and there is still a wave above the raft and we can't come out of this. Water comes over the front, the sides—it is in my chest, in my eyes. And then the wave breaks off, beneath the raft. And we rise higher still and I throw myself onto the bow of the raft, reach for the top D-ring, send my chest, my weight, every part of me, over the front. I think we are stuck, not going up or down. And then—

We fall forward. The bow of the raft is past the wave, beyond the roaring and foam. The river has let us go.

He sprawls in the bottom of the raft, his hat over his face, gripping his paddle in one fierce hand, nearly swimming in the swamped raft. I struggle out of the pool of water and stand on the tubes as the raft speeds away, raise my paddle to the sky and scream—sounds that aren't words, trying to outshout the falls but mingling with and lost in it. We bob downstream, facing the falls, and dance like madmen on the tubes until the raft swings around the corner to the Nahlin . . .

———

In a quarter mile we came to the confluence with the Nahlin. The knife edge of the ridge separating the two rivers came to a fine, high point, blocking our view upriver. We couldn't see the Nahlin until we were on it, and when we were on it we were on the first blue water since Chutine Lake. Across the river was a shack with a tiny eddy in front. We didn't know what this place might be—it hadn't been on the short list of details I owned—but we were exhausted. I wasn't interested in searching; any camp would do.

We struggled to make it across the river, and beached, and stumbled up the slope, and made camp in what amounted to the front yard of the deserted shack, and cooked, and got caught in a brief rainstorm; then it was dark.

11 *Take-Out*

Eventually, all things merge into one, and a river runs through it. The river was cut by the world's great flood and runs over rocks from the basement of time. . . . I am haunted by waters.

    —Norman Maclean, *A River Runs Through It*

That night on the shore of the Nahlin I had no more ambitions. I was settled, done—maybe not satisfied, just tired. We had run rapids all day, passed the biggest, and now there was a stillness. Before, in Wrangell in '86, on the Stikine in '88, back in Maine, or even on the Chutine, I'd been pursuing some ghost of Sid. As we'd run the rapids of the Sheslay, that phantom had gradually faded into the whitewater, and now it was gone. Not a stirring, not a sound.

———

In the morning I was so sore I couldn't move—tried to make myself but still couldn't. I awoke for a moment, blinked a few times, then fell back into sleep. When I rolled over, I realized how tender every part of me was, including my left arm, where the melanoma had been cut out; the scar had healed, but it continued to ache.

Later I was able to pull on some pants and groan into a freshly washed morning—rain had fallen off and on all night. Now it was blue and light. It felt like autumn, even though the date was only July fifteenth. The fifteenth: the day before had been Pat's birthday. Good idea not to drown on her birthday. A present, of sorts.

Max was already up, for once. We scuffled around, too grouchy to speak. I looked upstream along the Nahlin, which is the Nahlin only to this point, where the Sheslay and the Nahlin together become the Inklin, a transformation that only a cartographer would understand. The hills were low, rounded, smooth. It was very different from the canyon we had been in, and it reawakened the desire that new terrain evokes. One sight of unfamiliar land, and instantly I wanted to be there.

But we were going the other direction, and we had about a hundred miles left. One hundred miles is a long ways by river, but that morning felt like an ending—the same kind of wistful close-of-things that comes in late summer, when tourist joints and swimming pools shut down, when summer romances end. We had passed the last whitewater barrier, and there were no more decisions to make. We would head west on the Inklin, then bump slightly north, then south, and west again, through the Taku Flats to Taku Lodge and fly out from there. A hundred miles and out. Simple.

I was entirely at ease. Sitting on an ammo box, next to a smoky fire, with a river nearby, and trees and hills in the condition God made them, was as familiar as sitting in my living room on any summer morning. Max was nearly through packing, with a measured and careful manner, as though he were performing a ritual. "Any regrets?" he asked suddenly.

I looked around, puzzled. "About what?"

"About the falls. We were going to go, then we weren't, then we were. . . . You must have some regrets."

"Oh, that." I yawned. "Yeah, I do."

"But you know, it was the right call."

"Think so? I'm not so sure. We probably should have done it."

"No, I mean for me—for me it was the right call. I got to thinking about my sons when you went back to look at it again, and I thought about how we had no cover—there was no one to help us if we dumped, and I realized I was beyond this—I don't need that sort of thing any more. So it was the right call, not to go."

I shook my head, unconvinced. "Maybe. Maybe I thought too much about it. I was stuck between the two—it's where I've been all my life, between two options, two lives. Maybe we should have gone; you know, given up on thinking it through and just done it. Screw thinking about it."

"Stop trying to control the situation?" he asked with a knowing smile. "Well, I still think you made the right decision."

I bounced a rock off the *Dunny*. "As I've always said, 'Let your guide be your conscience.'"

"Wow. Deep."

I found my river clothes. They were soaking; my river bag had sprung a leak, and I'd been too lazy to patch it. "What should we call it?" I asked, pulling on sopping pants.

"How about Farewell Falls?" Max answered over his shoulder as he peed on a spruce. "We're leaving here, and you're through with guiding, right? So, 'Farewell.'"

I winced. I thought about the falls, about what the run would have been like. A good place to end my guiding life. I waited for regrets to come but felt only a slight tug. Maybe Max was right, and I hadn't been an idiot.

We stood around by the raft as though waiting for a benediction to be said, as though solemn words were needed. When none came we tossed our bags in and launched: once more into the foam.

Max tied a lure to one of our paddles to do some trolling, since he was sick of my food—"I'm sure sick of your food," is what he said—and we hadn't gone a quarter mile before the paddle and line shot out of Max's hands as though they had been tied to a jet. The line left a bloody trail as it ripped across his fingers.

"Whew," said Max, shaking his hand.

"What happened? Is it a fish?" I asked, looking around for the paddle.

"No, the lure must have got stuck on the bottom."

I kept looking around. "Where's the paddle?"

"It's gone," Max said. "That was a big lure."

"Oh great," I huffed. "Now we've got three paddles for a hundred miles." Max was contrite. "Sorry," he said.

After that the river straightened, running fast. Max guessed five miles an hour. I shrugged. It didn't matter anymore. In early afternoon we entered a long burn, where the left side had burned completely and the right had been scorched. A strange, apocalyptic area.

A grizzly walked upstream on the left shore about ten feet above the water. We steered in close to him. He suddenly stopped and looked out over the water at us, startled by this apparition. We were so close as we floated by that we could see the frown on his forehead. He crouched into a defensive position. He reared back on his hind legs, then dropped forward and came closer to the bank, sniffed the air, woofed and bent low in a crouch, and started to come down the bank toward us, but when we got too close he was gone like a ghost.

The river left the burn and reentered a deep green forest. Hardwoods and some evergreens shaded the river. The day was a mix of sun and clouds and no rain, an easy day to deal with. As we passed beside trees of the deepest green, and ferns beneath them at the river's edge, and the water swirling slowly, I was suddenly somewhere else—along the Rogue near Battle Bar—and it suddenly became all the rivers. How odd it seemed to have spent so much of my life, parts of eighteen years, living on rivers. So many days, so many afternoons of glinting sun, nights of shooting stars, mornings of feathery dew. Perhaps it was the lush cool of the shade on the south shore of the Inklin or the way the river stretched into a line and the current carried us along as though we were the current, and we just went, went, and went, but it made me feel lucky. The memory of all the rivers was there before me, an elastic chain of memories stretching out, dappled with bits and pieces of the experience of moving water: the shades of the river and shore, the texture of the day, the quality of the light, the colors, the feelings, sensations, moments. I looked around and remembered it all.

We saw two moose: a young male and a bull. Neither of them seemed too troubled by us, until we got to where they could smell us, then they bolted. I couldn't blame them. At midafternoon I didn't know where we were on the map, but I didn't care. We had enough food, enough time. The paddling was easy and I was drifting, far away and back, away and back. A classroom, a deep eddy, my wife, an eagle. We came to a sharp right-hand turn where the canyon opened and a broad gray drainage came in from the left: the Sutlahine River. It flushed into the Inklin in a wash, as unmistakable a marker as one could possibly get. And no one was there. Both that drainage and this were empty. I could see for miles up that one, to the headwater peaks of the Inklin Range. Rounded mountains, with snowfields running down them in thin stripes. Somewhere out there were other people, but only somewhere—and not many.

For a while I listened to the sound that glacier-milk makes against the raft, a sound like crushed ice tumbling in a drink or like a wave retreating from shore and trying to drag the sand with it. Against the raft it made a low hissing, a background noise that I would not hear unless I listened for it, and there it would be.

I heard a phrase in my head, something I'd read before leaving Maine: "Man is not at home in an interpreted world." It kept repeating itself with each dip of my paddle into the inky river, as though it were an important message I wasn't getting.

The Inklin branched out around low sandbars littered with the trees that had been washed down the Sutlahine. There were a million channels to choose from but no camps, so we slid across bars that barely had enough water to float us, as we tried to work our way to shore. A few miles downstream from the confluence, we reached the right-hand shore and parked. The canyon was beginning to cloud over, so we threw up our tent and Max's rain fly.

I started a fire and went off to gather more wood. The sandbar was covered with downed logs, and the driftwood that was wedged into the roots of any one of the trees would have kept a campfire going for a week. Driftwood lay all over the valley, and the walls of the canyon were covered in thousands, millions of trees. I couldn't exhaust this supply of driftwood in several lifetimes of cooking fires, and that was a cheering thought.

We huddled under the tarp during a rain shower, cooking and peering up and down the river. The rain moved in sheets and squalls, in low clouds that drifted down the canyon, then cleared to reveal the sides and tops of the canyon walls. It didn't last long; then, like God's sign to Noah, a tremendous rainbow appeared upstream, bridging the confluence of the Sutlahine and Inklin. Clouds lifted and let us see more and more of the canyon, but the rainbow stayed on. As the clouds fled, the birds began calling again. Max whistled once, and for a long time after, a songbird returned the call.

We were reduced to talking in half phrases, grunts—"Hot pan."

"Umm. Bitching rainbow."

"Look at this"—pointing at a bird nearby.

"Huh. Finch?"

"Warbler."

The rainbow lasted for almost an hour, shifting toward the west a little at the end. By then the day was starting to edge toward darkness, and I went for a stroll along the shore, among the gravel and driftwood, singing a capella some of the songs we'd used to sing when I was a guide. A Lovin' Spoonful song ("Taxman"), a Dylan ("It's All Over Now, Baby Blue"), and the theme song from *Gilligan's Island*.

I sang, working myself into a nostalgic funk, both for the time when I'd first sung these songs and for the mountains and rivers of interior British Columbia. I returned to the fire, where Max was sitting with a cup of tea, and played on the Jew's harp for a while and talked with Max about the glories of the evening.

"What are you going to do when we get out?" I asked him.

He shrugged. "Collect unemployment," he said.

I laughed. "Christ, you've become a guide. Next thing, you'll develop a drinking problem and your girlfriend will dump you." He flinched a little at that.

I taught him how to play the harp and built the fire high, in celebration of the abundance we were in the midst of. There were still spectacular clouds downstream, and the sky turning blue overhead—looked like it might even star up, and I expected a sliver of a moon to appear somewhere.

The sun set through the canyon downstream, between two hills that defined the direction of the river. It lit up the bottoms of the clouds in rose and purple and focused intense golden light on the hill behind our camp. Messages from an interpreted world: first the rainbow and now this blessing, lambent light.

At ten p.m. the canyon was misty and mysterious. At three a.m., when I got up, the canyon was entirely fogged in, as the clouds had dropped to the surface of the river. I could barely see it.

———

I am a slave to the memory of waters. Even if I wanted, I couldn't stop them. They are too vivid and too much connected to other things—being young, mostly—to fade. The images are of everything, but they all start from water, rivers. Then they extend outward, to the shore, the beaches, the guides, the canyons, then farther still to the roads leading to rivers, then to the places we lived and the things we did when we weren't on rivers.

A beach on the Rogue, a small sandbar just upstream from Kelsey Creek, where the river has slowed, a good place to take a swim in midafternoon;

the beach is an exquisite image, filled with deep shadows, water moving in a million different directions, and warm sand. The sand on my feet is comforting, the water is cool shade and a deep green in the sunlight, the sky is the right blue for a hot summer day. Boulders across the way, a tangle of trees, as much variety there as in the rest of the universe.

Watching a fellow guide floating up to the edge of Clavey Falls, and realizing he wasn't wearing a life jacket, and yelling out to him, and the despairing look that came over his face when he caught what I was saying, and him knowing then that it was too late for him to put it on before he was sucked over the falls.

An afternoon on the Middle Fork, looking downstream at the slopes of the canyon, in particular at an avalanche chute that had been sliced through the trees. There were ponderosa pines along the river, a few fallen on shore, and the river was as clear as air; in deep holes I could see cutthroat trout swimming, twitching in that irregular spasm of fin and tail. Morning on the Tuolumne, discovering two rattlesnakes engaged in a mating dance, uplifted on their tails on an outcropping of rock, writhing around each other in a living caduceus that wound on and on. It was both sensuous and disturbing, as the snakes undulated and flicked their tongues and hissed.

They are sharp memories, as crisp as a clean photograph, and even the edges are etched in: the trees off to one side, the rocks alongshore. The power surprises me, too. I can bring back the entire day, the exact temperature, the way the light hit the water of a waterfall and the feel of the water on my ankles, and the sensation of a day spent in shorts in a river in the woods, alternating between peaceful passages and the rush of whitewater.

Theologians, artists, scholars, bank tellers—everyone wants to know what makes life valuable. Sometimes I think it is the strength of one's memories that makes life worth the trouble. Perhaps I cherish my memories too much, like a small-souled miser who hoards his dollars, counting and recounting them. I drift through my treasury while staring out the den window; something prompts the flood of visions, but I can't say what. It can be a similar scene, or a glimpse of a bird or a branch, or of leaves scuttling, that leads me to other visions, and I'm off: a crisp morning in August on the McCloud in northern California, the tundra on the plains around the Noatak in August, the crystal quality of a July morning at put-in at Boundary Creek. The look of the water spilling out of Fall Creek in Mule Creek

Canyon on the Rogue in very late afternoon; drifting into a saving, soothing shadow along the Colorado in Grand Canyon; the deep, perfect green of the pines at Brushy Bar or at Little Soldier Creek on the Middle Fork; the smell of oak blowing across clear water on the Tuolumne in late afternoon; the tremendous empty distance after passing through Kobuk Canyon on the Kobuk; the sound of water, water, water . . .

———

The sun broke through the evanescent clouds around us, but huge misty ones still hung in, like the clouds in a Dali painting, suspended at many levels. Miles ahead were the famous Taku winds, strong winds blowing up the Taku River. We had been warned about them. Otherwise, there was nothing for us to worry about, except for my gloom at the thought of leaving. I was ready to head back to the Stikine and float down from Groundhog Jackson's.

When we left camp it felt as though we were chasing beauty. There had been so many exotic colors in the clouds downstream the night before that I expected to find some absurdly fantastic spot right around the corner. When we turned the corner, it was lovely, but lovely in a normal way. The Sutlahine had drained a valley running from south to north, and the Inklin was working its way north also, seeking a way through the coastal mountains, mountains with lofty titles, such as King Salmon Mountain and Mount Headman, but also Mount Lester Jones.

We came to a narrow canyon with a nice set of standing waves. We paddled right through the center of them, and all of a sudden we could smell rich green smells blowing upstream. The vegetation was different: ferns and broadleaf plants, coastal not interior. Max spotted a mountain goat high on the side of the canyon, and we craned our necks upward as we got deeper into the range. Some hills had rocky plateaus, bright green swards of trees, then a treeless slope above, dotted with snowfields looking bitterly cold.

After fifteen miles or so, the winds picked up, a precursor of the notorious Taku winds. They were so strong at times that I was afraid they might tip us over. We hunkered down in the raft, trying to keep our weight as low as possible. We struggled ahead through the wind for about an hour, and the river gradually bent to the left, which meant we were heading toward the confluence with the Nakina.

In late afternoon we came upon an old trapper's cabin on the right bank. We paddled into shore to examine it. Small and windowless, it was built of logs with moss chinked in between. It seemed like a lonely spot to spend time, far away from anyone else in the world.

But then Max said, "Hey, look," as he pointed across the river.

I turned and was surprised to see a lodge hanging over the river, directly behind me. "Whoa," I said. "What's that doing here?"

The lodge looked like someone's cute home, with curtains and a little flower garden, and I thought there would be an elderly man and his sweet-natured wife there. We paddled across to a beach downstream from the main building, where an aluminum boat was beached. There was a sign on the lodge — "Taku Safaries."

As we floated up, we saw a dog and a young man with his back turned to us. The dog started barking, and when the young man turned around, he did one of the best double takes I've ever seen. He looked, then he flinched, and then he looked again and dropped what he was holding and called the dog, and when our raft hit shore, he was chanting, "Holy shit, holy shit."

While he stood there saying "holy shit" to himself, another man appeared. He was in filthy jeans, low-slung on his skinny hips and open at the fly, with a black t-shirt, out of which skinny white arms stuck, with a big blue tattoo of a dragon on one. He had on a Taku Safari hat, covering stalks of straw-colored hair. Several inches of goatee dropped from his chin. His eyes were set wide apart and were a pale blue, and his skin was surprisingly sallow, considering where he lived.

He came down to the beach, looking puzzled as could be. "Where the hell did you come from?" he asked. "Upriver," Max said, nodding in that direction. That seemed to be all he wanted to know, and he invited us in for coffee.

He was Robbie and the kid was Eric. Robbie was the hunting guide for the outfitter who owned the lodge. Inside the lodge were coffee cups arranged underneath calico towels, and curtains on the windows, all very homey and domestic. We talked for nearly two hours in a dining nook that extended out toward the river. Or rather, Robbie talked. Eric, a high school student from Vancouver Island, hardly got a word in, but neither did Max or I. Listening to Robbie was like listening to a windstorm. As with most guides, he swore with passion and regularity. Every third or fourth word was "fuck" or one of its cognates, such as "fucking" or "fucked" or a hyphenated version: "fucking-cocksucking-son-of-a-bitch."

The stories ran together, a seamless river of tall tales. Much of what he said had to be true but was so mixed with self-promotion that it was hard to tell which parts were which. He told stories about hunting with a member of the Rothschild family who insulted him, and so Robbie walked away and left the French nobleman on a British Columbia hillside; about a picture he'd taken of two bears screwing; about a hunter he'd guided once who could hit a target at three hundred yards every time but couldn't hit a ram no matter how close Robbie brought him to it; about busting his brother in the mouth, so the brother had to eat with a straw; about how he used to be into Harleys, and how a judge had given him the choice of going to jail for three months or going to work for an uncle of his who was an outfitter; about having had three wives, and how he had advertised with a mail-order bride company to have someone come live with him — no takers; about the fish he'd caught on the first cast in this area — hundreds if not thousands; about the many records he had in Boone and Crockett.

Robbie brought out some smoked salmon and cookies and more coffee. After a while I got feeling so wrinkled and dry and hot inside the lodge that I longed for the river again, but it was hypnotic listening to Robbie. He never stopped, never paused. He and Eric were lonely for company, for anyone different, but Max and I had grown accustomed to our silent companionship — we weren't ready yet to let others into our world of two.

Max and I began making signs of restlessness and started the long process of excusing ourselves. First Robbie and Eric wanted to show us the grounds, which included several small cabins; then Max and I edged our way toward the *Dunny*, which looked faithful bobbing there at the landing, waiting for us. We shook hands all around and shoved off. The dogs circled and sniffed, then followed us downriver.

I shook my head in amazement. "Jesus Christ," I said. "Have you ever heard such bullshit?"

"A classic," agreed Max.

"Nice enough guy, though," I added, remembering that he had just shared his food with us.

We floated around the long, slow turn to the right below the lodge, while the dogs ran along and barked, and then we hit the real Taku wind. It was a steady bluster with occasional brutal bursts. For its roar to be so sustained didn't seem possible—but it was. The wind slowed us to a crawl, a stall, even though the current of the river was as strong as it had been upstream.

About twenty minutes later we heard an engine, the sound of a jet boat coming down from the lodge. "Oh no," groaned Max, "more stories." Robbie and Eric pulled alongside. "You want to see some rock art?" Robbie yelled. Without waiting for an answer he went on, "We'll mark the channel with a red tag for you." They roared off again and disappeared downriver. Minutes later they came back, waved, and headed toward the lodge.

The more we paddled, the more irritated with Max's paddling I became. He had been solid in the rapids, but now every half a minute or so he sighed, lifted his paddle out of the water, and laid it on the front of the raft while he looked around. That I continued to paddle against the howling wind meant nothing to him. "Keep paddling, Bud," I'd tell him in a light, amused voice from time to time, although I felt more like strangling him.

Lurching and twisting in the wind, we made our way around the corner to the flag. It marked the end of a backwater channel. We worked up it, then up another, even slower one. The carvings were at the point where the channel came closest to the rock wall on the outside of the river. It was a perfect camp, protected from the wind, which had been blowing hundreds of years before in exactly the same way as it was that day, and sheltered from rain as well.

The petroglyphs were high on the wall and had been dulled by wind and rain and sun. There were only three symbols carved into the rock that we could see: a ship with people; a serpentine figure, either of the river or of a snake; and a radiant sun image. I could feel how the picture-makers had reached forward in time through their pictures, and I wondered what symbols I would carve into a rock if I had a story to tell. Probably a river, a boat—probably a family.

We paddled for another hour in our fitful way, and the river broadened considerably, taking channels over and around gravel bars and trees. The river drifted wildly across the valley, then was checked by cliffs of banded and twisted sandstone. Beyond were the mountains, light and dark green, with streaks and fields of snow at the top. Sinwah Mountain and Chakluk, Shana, Hedron, and Lester Jones again.

About five miles past the Nakina, we began looking for a camp in earnest. We knew we had only another night or two out, so we were looking for a sublime spot, one that would keep up the string of ennobling locations we'd had. We became less choosy as the afternoon faded, but there weren't any places that would do. Making progress from island to island through the wind wasn't easy, as we moved in slow motion from one inadequate spot to the next. An island with a downed cottonwood on its downstream side appeared on the left. Slightly higher than the other islands in the area, it had a fifteen-by-forty-yard patch of dry sand at its center, so we stayed. The cottonwood provided something of a barrier, and we took the *Dunny* entirely out of the water and propped it against the cottonwood for a wind shield.

"Quite the wind," I said to myself as we worked.

"This sucks," Max added, an unusual complaint from him, being more inclined to stoicism in the face of weather.

When we had the camp set up, we found ourselves trapped: by the island we were on, by the wind, and by the sense of the trip winding down. The wind prevented our leaving the area for very long because an especially strong gust might take away the raft, the tent, the kitchen. We put together a big dinner, throwing caution to the raging wind because we saw the end clearly in sight. In two days, no more, we'd be in the vicinity of Taku Lodge or Juneau. We gorged on two packages of pudding and farted relentlessly afterwards. I wrote my notes Hemingway fashion, standing up, notebook resting against the top tube of the *Dunny*, and facing the wind, which ripped through my beard.

I felt like a river man again, as though I should go on from this river to the next to the next, seduced by currents. Yet we had passed a significant moment: Taku Safari and its implications. We were no longer Out; we were starting to come In—it would be a magnet now, the pull of settled places such as Juneau. Depressing.

The wind was ferocious. It roared, whipping the tent about. It almost forced me to retie everything in camp, for I was afraid that our gear would blow right off that pitiful little sandbar. But I didn't; we had done our best to cinch down the camp, and either it would blow away or it wouldn't.

Between gusts I thought of what being in Maine would be like. I would miss the simplicity of having very specific things to worry about—would the wind sweep our beach clean?—and the type of control I had over them:

to lash everything down better. My life would be different from this, soon, in ways I couldn't even imagine. I was looking forward to the baby, I knew I was, though thinking of how much my life would change worried me. I feared routines, restrictions; mostly I feared the very real possibility that I wouldn't be a good parent.

I wondered if this was the end of rivers for me. Sid's last trip had been when he was seventy-nine; I was only thirty-eight. Perhaps there was hope. And once again, for the thousandth time, I couldn't isolate, precisely, what the attraction had been, why I'd kept coming back to rivers and guiding in my mid twenties, then early thirties, and now again in middle age. I'd never been able to explain it, to myself or to others. Perhaps the explanation was destined to take its place among the other ineffable things, the reasons why the currents in a river morph in the way they do, why a combination of colors in a tree seems exquisite, why there is any thing rather than no thing, why the universe needs rivers.

I was sure there would be no long trips like this again for me and that my days of searching out new waters were probably over, as they'd been for Sid at about the same age. At that moment it was an abstract regret, since I was there, on a tiny patch of sand alongside the Taku, surrounded by wind. But I knew there would come a time, a winter day, when I would look out an office window on campus and see the Chutine snaking past Mt. Barrington, and be lost.

———

I am wearing my wool shirt and river shorts and flip-flops. It is early morning and I have just gotten out of my bag at Clavey, Whistling Bird, Shark's Mouth, Cliffside, Doe Creek, at Joe Bump, Elk Bar, North Fork, Hancock, and peed into the bushes. The sun strikes the top of the canyon on this morning in June of '77, July of '86, August of '90, May of '83, April of '73, September of '76. I smell water, see morning birds go from branch to branch, feel the sand on my feet. Time to build a fire.

———

The last full day was a slow blur. It disintegrated as time passed, as though we were hallucinating. The day seemed to have nothing to do with us, as though we drifted through it and through the fierce winds.

The early sky was filled with long, striated clouds, which nearly let in sun but not quite, and with the wind it was cold, and we would probably be wet and colder soon. For the first time, I put on my wool balaclava. The sun did break through occasionally on the hills to the west, which made them explode in color, backed as they were by the dark clouds. Again I was losing something—it was impossible to hold onto that fantastic color; it would always be impossible to hold onto such things.

We tried to head out earlier than usual, complaining about the wind without much enthusiasm ("This fucking wind," Max said. "Yeah," I agreed, "fucking wind."). We planned on making the border that day if possible; we didn't know if it would be. Robbie had said that the wind would die twenty miles from the lodge: not more, not less, exactly twenty miles, he said. Typical Robbie.

The clouds stayed low, seeming to wet us without actually raining, and the wind stayed, and we were as cold as we had ever been. The only compensation was the mountains. Wonderful mountains, dark gray, straight up, with a little bit of green on the bottom and partway up, then ice and snow and waterfalls in the valleys, and above them, the hanging valleys. It was the kind of view I would usually find powerful, but I had to work to remind myself that this was impressive, magnificent, the likes of which it is hard to come by. Then when my vision cleared I saw the mountains afresh and was in awe.

After a silent lunch we began seeing signs of people, especially as we entered the tighter portions of the coastal range. We came around one corner below a steep green mountain that seemed filled with water frozen or falling, and we encountered a drift net, another shocking sign of reentering the world. A fisherman was there, working with his wife. They pulled sockeye salmon out of a net, slit the salmons' gills, and tossed the fish in a bucket to bleed. They weren't surprised to see us.

For a long time after that, we were in sight of a smooth cleft in the rocks through which a thunderous waterfall was coursing, water bursting exuberantly off the wall and clouds masking the highlands from which it came. As we approached the border, the clouds dropped lower and lower, until they were right on top of the water, leaking on us. There was nothing left to see; the river was slow and insipid; and even the wind—which at least gave us an opponent, an adversary, an obstacle—had died, exactly where Robbie said it would. And now we were just paddling and drifting in the rain and fog. A dark time. We lifted our paddles, the water dripped off them into the river, we plunged the paddles back in, the blades disappeared into the water.

We came to another fishing camp, where an entire village seemed to be out on the water. We floated down on them, hearing their shouts and cries and curses well in advance of seeing them, as the fog had deepened and we appeared out of it like feeble spooks. We drifted between the boats, pulling up alongside to talk. After we left them and crossed the border stripe cut in the trees, we swung around an execrably slow bend and stopped on one pathetic little bar for a camp, but it was hopeless. No shelter, no wood, no decent place to put a tent. We went on.

The fog turned into heavy rain, and finally we just stopped. The trees all around spilled water, and everything we touched was wet. The river was nearly taken from view by the fog and rain, and the entire scene was dripping with *Hamlet*-ish gloom. Our spirits were flat. We were sloppy about everything. We let ourselves get wet in our rain gear, cooked a mushy and tepid meal on a sputtering stove, allowed rain into the tent, slept on a root all night, and disintegrated in the gloom. If we had still been in the bush— and we clearly no longer were—we would have been more careful; if we had been in the bush in our present mood, we might have expired on some gravel bar in a fit of ennui.

We woke to the same weather. We loaded as quickly as we could. The end had come, and one wants to be done with the end when the end has come. We wadded up our soggy gear, assuming we wouldn't need any of it that night, and dragged it all through the mud and brush down into the *Dunny*, which was a pitiful, soggy, muddy sight. I felt sorry for her, so we made an attempt to pump her up.

Only five or six miles to go: a slog down the river to the lodge and out.

"Ready?" I asked Max after we had thrown our gear into the raft.

"One more time, eh?" he said with a chuckle, for he had suddenly gotten happy. Maybe because we'd be off the river that day or because he'd be away from me then or because he'd be on his way to Katrina. He wasn't telling.

The character of the land was lost to me, hidden by fog as well as by the fog of my mind. After a long morning, the clouds burned off, and I expected to see the lodge around every corner. The current faded on us, and there

was a stiff upstream breeze still blowing—not a Taku wind but a steady
breeze working against us.

Max had become almost useless as a paddler. He would stroke once or
twice, then lay the paddle across his lap as though he were done with it
forever. The current had faded to a thread of moving water hiding alongshore, and I constantly moved us around, trying to stay in it while the wind
pushed us out of it, and I had to correct for Max every time he dropped his
paddle. The little cleft I get between my eyebrows deepened into a canyon
of disapproval, making a sore spot in my head. For the first time I felt the
effect of paddling on my shoulders and arms.

And the river kept going. The lodge was supposed to be at the point
where the river met the inlet. The current would have died there, and we
might even be bucking an incoming tide. A blue-gray-white thing came
into view high on the right side. As we slowly crept around the corner, the
blue-gray-white thing became the top slope of a glacier. It could only be
Twin Glacier, one of the largest in Alaska, an icefield covering hundreds of
square miles in the Boundary Mountains. We should have been at the lodge,
since the lodge was directly across from the glacier, but still the river bent
to the left, the wind blew, and the current continued to disappear. In fact,
it seemed we had reached the ocean tidal flow, forcing us back upriver, as
though the river wouldn't let us go.

As we got closer to the glacier, we heard tiny buzzing sounds, like distant
chainsaws. Then I realized it was planes, still so far off that they looked like
mosquitoes zipping back and forth across the front of the glacier. It was
a scene from an old war movie—an absurd sortie of single-engine planes,
going one way across the front of the glacier, then circling back the other
way. I expected to see tiny explosions as the lilliputian squadron bombed
the glacier.

We paddled for what seemed like several mornings, several afternoons—
the same strokes, the same wind, the same current fading, disappearing,
reappearing elsewhere, the same curve to the left, planes dropping and lifting and turning and buzzing all around us. The corner finally ended, and a
dock with a row of planes tied to it appeared. Taku Lodge at last.

⌒⌒

We tied up at one end of the dock and tried to improve ourselves. I took
off the bandana I always wore under my baseball hat, stuffing it into my

pocket, while Max ran his fingers through his wispy hair, then replaced his cap.

We went up to the lodge. It was like being in a theme park: Alaska Lodge Park. The employees were dressed up in period costumes, although what period it was I couldn't tell. The lodge was lovely, though—a log cabin and a thick emerald forest growing all around it, at every place where the will of man hadn't intervened. The floors inside were wide boards, and there were dead bears and dead moose lying about and huge picture windows facing the glacier.

Max and I were clearly out of place among the tourists in slickers and neat hair, and soon someone came up and gave us an inquiring look. I asked to see Ron Maas, the owner of the lodge. A woman dressed in Kansas gingham, I guessed, took us in back to the kitchen, where there was a booth filled with people who weren't in costume. An older man with a thick white beard, smoking a pipe, looked up from a pile of papers and receipts and introduced himself as Ron Maas.

"I'm Mike Burke and this is Max Sodalis," I said, thumb toward Max. "Did you hear we were coming?"

"No," Ron said, raising his eyebrows. "I didn't hear anything about it. Where'd you fellows come from? And sit down, have some salmon." He cleared a place at the booth for us. "Jenny, get a couple plates of salmon for these fellows, would you?" he called out to one of the many people in the kitchen.

Soon we each had a salmon steak and a big mug of coffee. We told Ron about where we'd been and the point of the trip.

"You know Sid Barrington, the riverboat pilot on the Stikine?" I asked.

"Oh sure, Barrington—I know his nephew Billy Barrington in Anchorage. Used to work with him in the shipping business."

"Well, Sid was a relative of mine, and I wanted to see the country he'd traveled in. I used to be a river guide, too, you see."

"Is that right?" Ron picked up a bank statement. "How was it?"

"Beautiful," I said. Nothing else came to mind.

Ron said we could catch a ride out on one of his empty planes but might have to wait until the next day. Max frowned at the news. We didn't have too many options, though, short of paddling the *Dunny* forty miles to Juneau on flat water.

Before we'd adjusted to this situation, it changed. One of the pilots came in to get his daily slab of salmon, and he said that the next group of planes, leaving in thirty minutes, would have room for us. This was good news, but we would have to break down our gear quickly, so we hustled down to the dock.

"Looks like we're going to make it," said Max happily as we walked.

"Yep, Juneau tonight," I agreed, having only a touch of regret at the thought of leaving the river. If Taku Safari was the beginning of being Out, Taku Lodge was truly Out—there was no point in staying any longer. The river had ended, and the river was what I had come for. In another mood I might have enjoyed Taku Lodge. Now, though, I just wanted to leave.

We packed the gear hastily and pulled the *Oyster Dunny* onto the dock so we could roll her up. The glacial milk on the tubes had dried and turned into dust, and I swept it off with my bandana; it was the least I could do for the *Dunny* after she had carried us faithfully. She hadn't given us any trouble since I'd patched her on the Stikine, and she had kept us afloat for nearly 225 miles and as far as I could tell was quite willing to carry us farther.

We loaded our gear into one plane and said goodbye to Ron Maas, who had come down to see us off; then Max and I crawled into another and flew to Juneau—I might have been interested in the scenery, excited by the glaciers, but I couldn't manage it. I had wanted to do this in a sea kayak. I fell asleep.

The plane skittered across the tops of some small waves to land in the harbor among the huge cruise ships docked there. We hauled our gear up a ramp, and I felt a transformation take place. I was Lord Byron all of a sudden: mad, bad, and dangerous to know. We went looking for a beer, and I caught a glimpse of myself in a window—in filthy blue climbing pants and gum boots, with a red rain jacket, a crusty black baseball cap, and glacier glasses—stomping up the street. Back from the Bush! Been out a long time! I'm Bad!

—————

I had to spend a few days in Juneau. I might have tried to change my flight to leave earlier, but I used the excuse of my reservation to delay, hoping something would come along that would conclude both the trip and my guide's life.

Max and I slept in a shack on Juneau Inlet belonging to a young woman, a friend of a friend of Max's. The shack was right on the water, at the end of a long, steep trail from the road, a trail that was nearly obscured by monstrous ferns. It had no running water, no heat, and no toilet; it was just one room with a peeling ceiling. We spread our sleeping bags on the floor, since our hostess, Nevett, hadn't appeared. In the morning we found her asleep on the couch, when we went to pee off the deck into the ferns.

That first morning I called Pat in Maine. She sounded eerily calm, at peace with herself. She wasn't. She'd been doing breathing exercises to keep anxiety attacks away. The baby was fine, though; indeed, it had kicked her so hard from inside that it had knocked a book off her lap. "How was the trip?" she asked.

"Well, it was good, I guess," I said, and, as with Ron Maas, I couldn't think of any more to say about it.

"When can you be back?" she wondered. I knew I couldn't wait much longer for a conclusion.

Max left that night to catch a ferry, after we had a few drinks at a bar and tried to relive the trip. We were pointed in different directions now, and I was looking forward to being alone, even though Max and I had found a way to get along; we had overcome our obvious differences, shared an experience, and were friends because of it. He asked if the trip had been what I wanted.

"You know, I'm not sure. I don't think I know what I really wanted, or what I thought would happen. But I got to see some places Sid saw, got to run some new water, had some laughs . . ." I shrugged.

"Well, that's okay, isn't it? You got something out of it, even if you don't know what it was, just like I did."

"Yeah? What'd you get?"

He spread his arms. "I got to be there. Thank you for that."

I was embarrassed. "My pleasure." I looked around at all the faces in the bar—so many faces, so strange to see them all gathered in one spot. "Well, I don't know what the point was, but it worked out anyhow, didn't it?"

Max grinned his dimpled grin. "You learned," he said.

We shook hands at the bar. Max headed for the ferry terminal, and I went off to watch over a dog, cat, and condo belonging to a friend of Nevett's for the next two nights.

Nevett loaned me her car, the ugliest, most beat-up VW bug in the world. Rusted out by the Alaskan winters, the VW's floorboards were gone; the seat rocked back and forth, unattached to the floor; and the transmission was missing fourth gear. I drove it into town, watching for cops, since none of its lights worked. I wandered, in bookstores and cafés and bars, waiting for my flight, and I found a copy of Barrett Willoughby's novel *River House* in an antiquarian bookshop. As I went around town, I found myself listening in, tuned to other people's conversations. I realized I was listening for their plans—for a ride, for a trip, for a way back into the bush. I shook my head. This wouldn't do.

The day I left, the clouds that had been dogging the city vanished and Juneau was glorious, with the mountains behind the city in the clear and waterfalls tearing off them, and already I was far away from the waterfalls at Chutine Lake, on the Stikine, the Taku. I sat on the condo's patio, in the sunshine, with the cat in my lap. I still felt as though I weren't done, that I'd missed the point. I read words of Sid's in Willoughby's book—"But this old Stikine—she's a child of glaciers. She's always got some new trick to spring on me. I love her. I have men aboard now who have been steamboating with me for nearly thirty years. They feel the same way about her. I watch her, and they watch her—every minute."

And then I was finally done, because finally I understood something: What I understood was the Stikine, a little, the Chutine and the Sheslay and the Nahlin and the Taku; I understood the Tuolumne and the Middle Fork and the Owyhee and Kobuk and Colorado and Kennebec and some small creeks in Mexico. What I knew was the Rogue and the Umpqua and the Main Salmon and the Green and the Noatak and the Tatshenshinni and Ambler, Skwentna, and Stanislaus.

Facing east, toward the waterfalls behind Juneau, toward Telegraph Creek and Maine, I saw what had been true before I left home and what was true now as I headed back. Everything important I would ever know about Sid's river life I already knew—what he had felt about life on a river was what I felt; the hold that rivers had on him was the same hold that they'd placed on me; the reasons why he kept going back were the same reasons I did.

After pursuing Sid through history, by river, in imagination, I arrived at this moment, the cat settled peacefully in my lap: I knew a little about rivers, and that was all I would ever need to know about Sid.

Winter 2005

There's nothing in the Big Book of Life that says you can't do this forever.
— Del Johns, river guide

My daughter, Harper, is now fifteen, a beautiful, healthy redhead who, when she was six, liked to say, "God is bigger than you are, Daddy." Every year she and I make maple syrup from the sap of our trees, and every year I work on our old house a little, improving, changing, molding it to some vision I have of the way things ought to be.

I haven't seen Max since 1991; the spoon he whittled is still on my desk, bleaching whiter each year. I know he moved to southern British Columbia, married the Russian, got divorced, married a German woman, and successfully raised his two sons; the last time I talked to him, he thanked me, again, for not running Farewell Falls on the Sheslay: "That was the moment when I realized I was beyond that stuff, that I was a father, not an adventurer."

I haven't been back to British Columbia or Alaska, but I imagine that Telegraph Creek has changed. I don't want to know what's happened to Chutine Lake or the Sheslay; such places can't be improved by changes. I still guide a trip or two in Idaho, on the Middle Fork, because I can't get away—from mountains, other guides, rivers. Every winter I begin to think of canyons, of beaches and eddies and rocks, and I feel the pull again, "the old fierce pull" of rivers. And so I ask Pat and she says "Go" and I go—for a week, for three, but I go.

I talked to an old-timer from Telegraph Creek a few years after the trip. He said of Sid that Barrington was "one of the finest riverboat men—it was a pleasure to be on the river with him. A wonderful man." One other thing the old-timer said about Sid has stayed with me: "He had one enemy," the old-timer said, "and that was himself."

There is a photograph of the *Hazel B. No. 3* hanging over the desk in my den. In it, Sid and Hill and Harry are standing by the wheelhouse, somewhere along the Stikine. Behind the *Hazel B.* are a mountain and low clouds. It is probably the early 1930s, and the three of them would be in their fifties. Sid, fittingly, is inside the wheelhouse with one hand on the wheel, while Hill and Harry frame him. Hill has a haunted, sullen expression; he wears a heavy denim jacket and a fedora and is standing directly beneath the ship's bell. His left hand is stuck into the buckle of his belt like a claw. Harry's smile is slight, beatific, the gentle expression of a favorite uncle. His right hand, covered by ground-in dirt, rests on the wheelhouse windowsill. The left hand is propped in a fist on his right hip. He is wearing a cardigan and a cap.

Sid, too, has a hat, but he is back in the shadows and so it is mostly his face that I see, a moon in the window. He looks impatient, but curious, too. His eyes are in a squint, and they have one or two dark shadows beneath each. His mouth is downturned at the corners, and two strands of his hair have fallen upon his forehead, looking exactly like scars.

One evening when she was two or three, Harper was crawling over me while I worked at the desk. She searched through the desk drawers, pulling out the junk gathered there. Tiring of that, she looked around for something else that would interest her, when she stood up on my legs, pointed, and said, "There you are, Daddy!" as though she'd gotten the answer to a question.

I looked up from my papers to see what she meant. "What?"

"There," she insisted, crawling off my lap and partway across the desk. She put her finger directly on the photograph. "There you are," she said, her finger on Sid's nose, pointing again and again at the swift-water pilot's image. "There you are, Daddy, there, there," she repeated, determined that it was true, determined to make it true, determined that I be Sid.

Suggested Reading

Abbey, Edward. *Down the River*. New York: Dutton, 1982.

Berton, Pierre. *The Klondike Fever: The Life and Death of the Last Great Gold Rush*. New York: Knopf, 1958.

Blaustein, John, and Edward Abbey. *The Hidden Canyon*. San Francisco: Chronicle Books, 1999.

Chapple, Steve. *Kayaking the Full Moon*. New York: HarperCollins, 1993.

Cox, Chana B. *A River West Out of Eden*. Lagunitas, Calif.: Lexikos, 1992.

Fletcher, Colin. *One Man's Journey Down the Colorado Source to Sea*. New York: Knopf, 1997.

Ghiglieri, Michael P. *Canyon*. Tucson: University of Arizona Press, 1992.

Gilliland, Judith. *River*. New York: Clarion Books, 1993.

Graves, John. *Goodbye to a River*. New York: Knopf, 1960.

Hoagland, Edward. *Notes from the Century Before: A Journal from British Columbia*. San Francisco: North Point Press, 1982.

Huser, Verne, editor. *River Reflections*. Chester, Conn.: Globe Pequot Press, 1985.

Johnston, Tracy. *Shooting the Boh*. New York: Vintage, 1992.

Kane, Joe. *Running the Amazon*. New York: Knopf, 1989.

Lavender, David. *River Runners of the Grand Canyon*. Tucson: University of Arizona Press, 1985.

McCairen, Patricia. *Canyon Solitude*. Tucson, Ariz.: Treasure Chest Books, 1998.

Meloy, Ellen. *Raven's Exile*. New York: Henry Holt, 1994.

O'Connor, Cameron, and John Lazenby. *First Descents: In Search of Wild Rivers*. Birmingham, Ala.: Menasha Ridge Press, 1989.

Powell, John Wesley. *The Exploration of the Colorado River and its Canyons*. New York: Penguin Classics, 2003.

Ryan, Kathleen Jo. *Writing Down the River*. Foreword by Gretel Ehrlich. Grand Canyon, Ariz.: Grand Canyon Association, 2004.

Sadler, Christa, editor. *There's This River: Grand Canyon Boatman Stories*. Flagstaff, Ariz.: Red Lake Books, 1994.

——— (primarily the work of Marty Loken). *The Stikine River*. Alaska Geographic Society, 1979.

Sturgis, Kent. *Four Generations on the Yukon*. Fairbanks, Alaska: Epicenter Press, 1988.

Teal, Louise. *Breaking into the Current*. Tucson: University of Arizona Press, 1994.

Thoreau, Henry David. *A Week on the Concord and Merrimack Rivers*. Princeton, N.J.: Princeton University Press, 1980.

Twain, Mark. *Life on the Mississippi*. Boston: James R. Osgood and Company, 1883.

Wallach, Jeff. *What the River Says*. Hillsboro, Ore.: Blue Heron Publishing, 1996.

Willougby, Barrett. *River House*. New York: Triangle Books, 1935.

———. *Sitka: Portal to Romance*. Boston and New York: Houghton Mifflin Company, 1930.

Zwinger, Ann. *Downcanyon*. Tucson: University of Arizona Press, 1995.

About the Author

For almost thirty-five years, Michael Burke has been a whitewater and wilderness guide, having run rivers in California, Oregon, Idaho, Alaska, British Columbia, Washington, Arizona, Utah, Maine, and Mexico. He first guided in Alaska in 1977 on the Noatak and Kobuk rivers, and in 1983 he made the first rafting descent of the Skwentna River in the Alaska Range.

Burke is a native of northern California and a graduate of the University of California–Berkeley, with a degree in philosophy (1977), and of the University of Massachusetts–Amherst with an MFA in English–creative writing (1984). He is an associate professor in the English Department at Colby College in Waterville, Maine, where he teaches environmental literature and writing, as well as subjects in American literature; he is also the director of the Honors Program at the University of Maine at Farmington. He has taught in London and Cape Town, South Africa.

Mr. Burke lives in Wilton, Maine, with his wife, Patricia, and daughter, Harper. In addition to Harper he has two older children: Emma and Brendan O'Donnell.